SANDWICHES

OF THE WORLD

RECIPES FROM 108 GREAT CHEFS

Photography by BATTMAN

Distributed in the United States by Battman Studios
New York, New York

Published by Battman Studios
Text and Photographs © 2007 by Battman
All rights reserved. Printed in China

ISBN 6-423118-80-5

www.battmanstudios.com

Book Design by Lisa Sragg: EnModa Design, New York
Editor: Stephanie R. Mercurio
Associate Editor: Fayeann L. Lawrence
Recipe Editor: Mark Vogel, foodforthoughtonline.net
Wine Consultant: May Matta-Aliah, www.red-dot-solutions.com

Front Cover Photograph: Anthos, New York
Back Cover Photograph: db bistro moderne, New York
Cover Photography: Battman

restaurants and chefs

Restaurant	Chef	Page
21 Club	John Greeley	166
A Voce	Andrew Carmellini	74
Amalia	Ivy Stark	4
Annisa	Anita Lo	88
Anthos	Michael Psilakis	148
	Jason Hall	148
Aquavit	Johan Svensson	130
Aureole	Tony Aiazzi	76
Babbo	Mario Batali	34
	Gina DePalma	34
Bar Jámon	Andy Nusser	154
Barbounia	Timothy Reardon	94
Beppe	Marc Taxiera	64
	March Walker	64
BLT Steak	Laurent Tourondel	172
Blue Smoke	Kenny Callaghan	106
Bouchon Bakery	Thomas Keller	126
	James Vellano	126
Café Boulud	Bertrand Chemel	58
Casa Tua	Sergio Sigala	18
Chanterelle	David Waltuck	6
Chef	Pierre Shaedelin	82
Chef	Wayne Nish	150
Citarella	Jeremy Culver	20
Craft	Tom Colicchio	48
	Damon Wise	48
Dante	Dante Boccuzzi	152
David Burke & Donatella	Eric Hara	176
David Burke at Bloomingdales	Chris Shea	78
David Burke Las Vegas	David Burke	90
DB Bistro Moderne	Daniel Boulud	46
DB Bistro Moderne	Olivier Muller	128
Devin Tavern	Derrick Styczek	146
District	Patricia Williams	28
District	Derrick VanDuzer	72
Dry Creek Kitchen	Charlie Palmer	8
Eighty One	Ed Brown	132
Emeril's	Emeril Lagasse	87
Emporium Brasil	Samire Soares	114
Flatiron Lounge	Julie Reiner	184
Fleur de Sel	Cyril Renaud	174
Gonzo	Vinny Scotto	142
Good Enough To Eat	Carrie Levin	70
Gramercy Tavern	Michael Anthony	144
Gusto	Amanda Freitag	84
Havana Blue	Richard G. Garcia	16
	José Rodriquez	16
Hawaiian Tropic Zone	Joel Reiss	162
Institute of Culinary Education	Andrew Gold	36
Jean Georges	Greg Brainin	68
Kefi	Michael Psilakis	134
L'Atelier	Joël Robuchon	40
	Yosuke Suga	40
Landmarc	Marc Murphy	14
	Frank Proto	14
Le Bernardin	Eric Ripert	140
Le Petit Chateau	Scott Cutaneo	86
Mai House	Michael Bao Huynh	102
Mandarin Oriental	Toni Robertson	52
Matsuri	Tadashi Ono	110
Metrazur	Michael Lockard	22
Millennium UN Plaza Hotel	Scott Owen	24
Mozzarelli's	Ron Malina	98
Mr. K's	Cheng-Hua Yang	50
	Nicholas Lee	50
Negril	Marva Layne	108
Nice Matin	Andy D'Amico	112
Nobu	Nobu Matsuhisa	160
Nobu NY	Ricky Estrellado	178
Norma's	Emile Castillo	180
Ouest	Tom Valenti	118
	Scott Varricchio	118
Pantry Raid Style	Michael Schulson	156
Pearl Oyster Bar	Rebecca Charles	80
Perry St.	Jean-Georges Vongerichten	60
Petrossian	Maggie Huff	96
Petrossian	Michael Lipp	104
Pine Hollow Country Club	Ari Nieminen	182
Porter House	Michael Lomonaco	138
Prince Street Cafe	Gary Volkov	158
Pulse	Jake Klein	100
Rock Center Café	Antonio Prontelli	10
Rocking Horse Cafe	Jan Mendelson	56
Shaffer City Oyster Bar	Jay Shaffer	12
	Kary Goolsby	12
Sueños	Sue Torres	136
Sushi Samba	Michael Cressotti	170
Taboon	Efi Noan	168
Tamarind	KB Singh	116
	Claudio Quito	116
Telepan	Bill Telepan	164
Thai Market	Tanaporn Tangwibulchai	44
The Children's Storefront	Stephen Alleyne	30
The Four Seasons	Christian Albin	92
	Fred Mero	92
	Peco Zentilaveevan	92
The Modern	Gabriel Kreuther	122
The River Café	Brad Steelman	120
The Waverly Inn	John DeLucie	42
	Nick Cataldo	42
	Domingo Gabriel	42
Tour	Kenneth W. Collins	124
Town	Geoffrey Zakarian	54
Trump Grill	Christopher Devine	32
Turbo Chef	Alison Brushaber	38
WD~50	Wylie Dufresne	62
'wichcraft	Sisha Ortuzar	26
Woo Lae Oak	Harold Soo Hyung Kim	66

What do Nobu, Daniel, Jean-Georges, Andrew Carmellini, Laurent Tourondel, Emeril and Charlie Palmer have in common? Besides a passion for creating delicious food, these chefs, along with all great chefs, are not known for making sandwiches. Flip though the pages of this book and you'll find some of the most wonderful, outrageous, simple, complicated and beautiful sandwiches by over 100 outstanding chefs from around the world. From a Korean sandwich wrapped in lettuce, to a Guatemalan influenced sandwich using popcorn, to the fanciest peanut butter and banana sandwich you have ever seen, this book will amaze you. The Earl of Sandwich (yes, there actually was one) could have never imagined what he had started. These recipes are also paired with a suggested wine. Just because you don't need a knife and fork (although a few could use their assistance), doesn't mean that these sandwiches couldn't be considered an entrée with a fine glass of wine.

BATTMAN | PHOTOGRAPHER

sandwiches

The practical aspect of eating food as a sandwich is simple and straightforward; various foods, encased between pieces of bread, or wrapped in a soft flatbread, can be easily picked up and brought to mouth without utensils, plate, table, or even a place to sit.

Most people know, at least vaguely, the story of John Montagu, the 4th Earl of Sandwich, who, while at the gambling tables of London in the 1700s, was first to put a couple of slices of roast beef between two pieces of bread to eat so he would not interrupt his gaming. Eminently practical guy he was. That is the story that has stuck, for today we all call the savory quick meals by his title. As an aside, the place name Sandwich, in Kent, meant "sand place" in Old English, a fact that may have some relevance to many of us who may remember getting sand in our peanut butter and jelly sandwiches while playing at the beach as children.

Fewer people know that some 800 years before, a Jewish leader named Hillel the Elder made the first sandwich ever recorded. He wrapped Passover lamb and bitter herbs in a soft matzoh to eat as a reminder to other Jews of their forced labor in Egypt. It quickly became popular. The Romans gave it a name: cibus Hilleli, or Hillel's food.

Later, during the Dark Ages, forerunners of modern dinnerware at banquets were trenchers: slabs of bread put on a table in front of a diner that served as plates on which roasted meats were served. When the meats were consumed, the trenchers which had become soggy with au jus, were either eaten, thrown to the dogs or given to the poor. These forerunners preceded the modern open-faced sandwiches of Scandinavia, and were possibly concurrent with Ethiopian injera, which is a flatbread on which food is served and eaten.

Today, the number of varieties of sandwiches around the world is staggering and their definitions are blurred. It seems every culture has one. New York City wouldn't be the same without corned beef and pastrami sandwiches on rye bread. American BLTs, club sandwiches, grilled cheese, hamburgers and hot dogs stand side by side with Mexican burritos, quesadillas and tacos, filled arepas from South America, steamed Chinese bao and bings, Vietnamese banh mi, pressed and cooked Italian panini, sandwich Cubanos, and unleavened wraps of all types seem to exist everywhere. This raises a question; are Vietnamese summer rolls with wrappers made from rice, deep-fried Chinese egg rolls and Southeast Asian spring rolls closer to sandwiches than dumplings? They begin life as wraps. And after all, a Monte Cristo is a sandwich, isn't it? Even if it's dipped in egg and then fried in butter. So is a Croque Monsieur, for that matter.

The sky's the limit. Have at it.

WAYNE NISH | CHEF

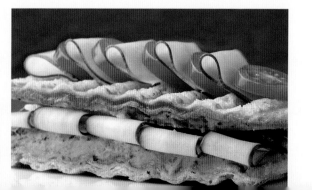

PAIRS WELL WITH

honey-rosemary lamb sandwich

YIELDS 6 SANDWICHES

INGREDIENTS

1 ½ lbs. ground lamb

1 yellow onion, chopped

2 cloves garlic, minced

1 Tbsp. harissa (Moroccan spice paste)

1 tsp. ground cumin

1 tsp. ground coriander

1 tsp. sweet paprika

2 cups puréed San Marzano tomatoes

¼ cup honey

2 tsp. finely chopped fresh rosemary leaves

Salt and pepper, to taste

6 semolina raisin rolls

6 pieces grilled radicchio

3 oz. fresh goat cheese

4 pepperoncini, sliced into rings

METHOD

In a large casserole dish over high heat, crumble lamb with a wooden spoon, stirring often until light brown, about 8 minutes. Remove meat with a slotted spoon and discard all but 1 Tbsp. fat from pan.

Return meat to pan. Add onion, garlic, harissa, cumin, coriander, and paprika. Stir occasionally until onion begins to brown, about 4 minutes. Add tomato purée, honey, and rosemary; stir occasionally until hot, about 2 minutes. Add salt and pepper to taste.

Set roll bottoms on plate and cover with radicchio leaves. Spoon lamb mixture over radicchio, crumble goat cheese over top with pepperoncini slices, and set tops in place.

amalia

EXECUTIVE CHEF

Ivy Stark

TERRACES
MARLBOROUGH
PINOT NOIR
BRANCOTT

grilled cheese
with white truffle butter

SANDWICH

6 Tbsp. (about 6 oz.) prepared white
    truffle butter, softened

8 slices good quality white bread, or brioche
    (*I use brioche pain de mie*)

6 oz. Italian fontina cheese, grated, (about ³/₄ cup)

4 Tbsp. butter

METHOD

Spread the truffle butter on the slices of bread, reserving enough to go on the outside of the sandwiches. Divide the cheese among 4 slices of bread and close the sandwiches with the other slices. Press down. Smear remaining truffle butter on the outside of the now closed sandwiches. Melt the regular butter in a large sauté pan. When just melted, place the sandwiches in the pan and cook over medium heat until browned, or the cheese is melted. Remove from pan, trim crusts and cut each sandwich into eighths diagonally, making little triangles.

Serve as a hors d'oeuvre along with little shots of tomato soup.

TOMATO SOUP   (yields about 5 cups)

1 medium Spanish onion, peeled and
    coarsely chopped

5 cloves garlic, peeled and coarsely chopped

3 Tbsp. butter

¼ cup brandy

3 pts. chicken stock or water

3 pts. canned plum tomatoes, including juice

3 Tbsp. tomato paste

1 cup basil leaves (stems are ok), washed
    and very roughly chopped

1 qt. heavy cream

Salt and pepper, to taste

Sugar, to taste

METHOD

Sweat the onion and garlic in the butter in a very large saucepot over medium low heat for about 15 minutes, until the onion is soft and translucent and not at all browned (add a splash of white wine if you need to slow down the process.) Add the brandy, and raise the heat to high, cooking off all the brandy, about 2-3 minutes. Add the stock or water, tomatoes, tomato paste and basil. Bring to a boil, reduce heat to medium. Simmer 30-40 minutes. Strain into another pot, return to heat, and boil for 5 minutes to further reduce. Add the cream and return to a boil. Boil for 5-10 more minutes, whisking often until soup is lightly thickened and tasty. Season with salt, pepper, and possibly a bit of sugar, if needed.

CHANTERELLE

EXECUTIVE CHEF
David Waltuck

smoked salmon & crisp potato-wich

with american caviar

YIELDS 1 SANDWICH

INGREDIENTS

32 potato slices, ⅛ inch thick,
    2½ inch diameter

1 cup clarified butter

Salt and pepper, to taste

4 oz. smoked salmon, sliced thin
    on a long bias

1 cup whipped crème fraiche

4 oz. American sturgeon caviar

1 red pearl onion,
    peeled and shaved thin

Dill sprigs, as needed

METHOD

Dry the potato slices a bit by pressing between a kitchen towel. Heat an 8 inch sauté pan with 1/4 cup of the clarified butter until just before smoking. Start adding the potatoes in a circular, overlapping pattern, making two layers. When the bottom layer has browned nicely, carefully flip and cook the topside, adding more clarified butter as needed. When lightly golden, remove from sauté pan to a tray lined with a few layers of paper towel and season. Repeat. Layer the salmon in between the two crisp potatoes with crème fraiche, caviar, red pearl onion shavings, and dill sprigs.

CHARLIE PALMER

DRY CREEK KITCHEN

NORTH SONOMA CO

EXECUTIVE CHEF
Charlie Palmer

JACOB'S CREEK®
CABERNET
MERLOT
VINTAGE

country ham
and italian pickled eggplant panini

requires advance preparation

YIELDS 4 PANINIS

INGREDIENTS

4 semolina hero rolls

6 oz. black olive tapenade (recipe follows)

6 oz. imported fontina cheese

1 lb. country ham, sliced thin

8 oz. pickled Italian eggplant (recipe follows)

6 oz. roasted red peppers (recipe follows)

DAVID BUICO'S PICKLED ITALIAN EGGPLANT

3 medium Italian eggplants, peeled and julienned

3 oz. kosher salt

4 sprigs fresh thyme

4 garlic cloves, smashed

1 oz. sugar

2 tsp. kosher salt

1 tsp. crushed red pepper flakes

3 oz. extra virgin olive oil

6 oz. white balsamic vinegar

ROASTED RED PEPPERS

6 red bell peppers

2 cloves garlic

Salt and pepper, to taste

Olive oil, as needed

BLACK OLIVE TAPENADE

½ lb. pitted black kalamata olives

1 oz. marsala wine

Salt and pepper, to taste

2 anchovies

3 oz. extra virgin olive oil

METHOD

Toss julienned eggplant with 3 oz. kosher salt. Place in a bowl and let sit for 24 hours refrigerated. Drain off all excess liquid and toss with remainder of ingredients. Place in mason jars well sealed for 14 days. Keep refrigerated.

Toss red peppers with the garlic, salt, pepper and olive oil. Roast at 450° for 10 to 12 minutes, or until the peppers start to blister. Remove from the oven and place in a bowl and cover with plastic wrap for 10 minutes. When peppers are cool enough to handle, peel, de-seed and julienne them. Mix them with the finished pickled eggplant.

In a food processor add all ingredients and puree till smooth.

To assemble, slice the semolina bread lengthwise leaving it attached on one side. Spread olive tapenade on both sides. Layer on the fontina cheese and ham. Top with pickled eggplant and peppers. Place in the panini machine and press till cheese is melted and bread is toasted.

ROCK CENTER CAFÉ

EXECUTIVE CHEF
Antonio Prontelli

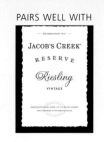

snapper ceviche finger sandwich
(deconstructed)

INGREDIENTS

2 lbs. skinless red snapper fillets,
    medium dice

1 medium red onion, small dice

1 yellow bell pepper, small dice

1 red bell pepper, small dice

1 jalapeno, small dice

¼ bunch cilantro leaves, chopped

Juice of 6 limes

Salt and pepper, to taste

Sugar, to taste

1 bag microwave popcorn

METHOD

Combine all of the ingredients, (except the popcorn). Cover with plastic wrap and place in the refrigerator for a minimum of 30 minutes and a maximum of 2 hours.

Pop the popcorn when ready to serve. Place the ceviche in individual bowls and serve the popcorn beside it.

If you are feeling adventurous, try and make the sugar/popcorn bread. Heat 1/2 cup of sugar in a sauce pot until it starts to melt and becomes a liquid. This will take place rather quickly. Pour the mixture onto a greased parchment paper. Sprinkle popped popcorn to the top of the sugar mixture. Allow to cool slightly and then cut into desired sizes.

CHEF / OWNER

Jay Shaffer

CHEF DE CUISINE

Kary Goolsby

pork cutlet sandwich

with fontina, tomatoes, cherry peppers and arugula

SANDWICHES of the WORLD

SERVES 4

INGREDIENTS

1 cup all purpose flour

3 eggs

2 cups plain breadcrumbs

½ cup grated Pecorino Romano cheese

4 boneless pork cutlets, pounded thin

¼ cup olive oil, for frying

1 bunch rocket arugula, washed well

8 pickled cherry peppers

Salt and black pepper, to taste

2 Tbsp. extra virgin olive oil

4 ciabatta rolls

3 Tbsp. mayonnaise

6 sun-dried tomatoes, soaked in warm
    water for 10-15 minutes

4 large slices fontina cheese

METHOD

Place flour in a shallow dish. In a separate shallow dish, beat the eggs. In a shallow dish, combine breadcrumbs and cheese. Dredge the pork in flour (to coat lightly), dip into the egg mixture, covering completely, and then into the breadcrumb mixture to coat the cutlet. Heat the oil in a large sauté pan on medium heat. Place the cutlets in the oil and fry until browned. Flip and cook on the other side for 2-3 minutes more, or until golden brown. Remove to a plate and rest on paper towels. Do not cover.

Toss arugula and cherry peppers with salt, pepper and extra virgin olive oil. Slice the ciabatta rolls in half and spread mayonnaise on the top half. Divide and place the arugula mixture on the bottom halves. Reserve.

Put cutlets on a cookie sheet and top with tomatoes and fontina cheese and put under the broiler until the cheese is melted, about 30 seconds. Place cutlet on top of arugula and pepper mixture and press to close.

LANDMARC

CHEF / OWNER

Marc Murphy

CHEF

Frank Proto

soft shell crab blt

SANDWICHES of the WORLD

SERVES 4

INGREDIENTS

4 live soft shell crabs (substitute
   frozen only if out of season)
1 ½ cups buttermilk
1 large egg
1 Tbsp. kosher salt
Fresh ground black pepper, to taste
Cayenne pepper, to taste
1 cup cornmeal
1 cup all-purpose flour
2 qts. peanut oil, for frying
   (or vegetable oil)
½ cup organic micro baby greens
Crispy chorizo chips
Oven dried tomato chips
Chinese mustard sauce

METHOD

To clean the crabs, remove spongy substance (gills) that lies under the tapering points on either side of the back shell. Place crab on back, and remove the small piece at lower part of shell that terminates in a point. Wash crabs thoroughly; drain well and dry on paper towels.

Whisk together buttermilk and egg, add the crabs, and soak for 15 minutes. In a shallow dish, combine salt, black pepper, cayenne, cornmeal, and flour. Reserve. In a large heavy skillet heat the peanut oil until very hot (approximately 350°).

Remove the crabs from the buttermilk, scraping off any excess buttermilk with your fingers. Dip the crabs in the cornmeal mixture and turn to coat. Carefully place the crabs in the skillet and cook until golden brown on both sides, turning once, about 3 to 5 minutes total. Transfer crabs to paper towels to drain.

St. Thomas, Virgin Islands

EXECUTIVE CHEF
Richard G. Garcia

CHEF DE CUISINE
José Rodriquez

CRISPY CHORIZO CHIPS

3½ oz. Spanish chorizo ham
   sliced into ⅛-inch rounds
Peanut oil, as needed

METHOD

Cook the chorizo in peanut oil for 2-3 minutes until lightly browned. Remove and drain on paper towels.

OVEN-DRIED TOMATO CHIPS

¼ cup Spanish extra virgin olive oil
1 Tbsp. high quality balsamic vinegar
Salt and fresh ground black
   pepper, to taste
2 Roma tomatoes, ends cut and
   sliced into ¼ inch rounds

Pre heat oven to 200°. Combine oil, vinegar, salt and pepper in a bowl and gently toss tomatoes being careful not to break the flesh. Let sit 5 minutes. Remove tomatoes from the marinade and place on a cooling rack sitting on top of a baking sheet and place in oven for about 1 hour or until the tomatoes have dried out. Tomatoes will crisp as they cool down.

CHINESE MUSTARD SAUCE

1 cup boiling water
4 Tbsp. soy sauce
1 cup dry mustard
¼ cup vegetable oil
Additional water as needed

Combine boiling water, soy sauce and dry mustard. Whisk together until a smooth paste. Slowly add the oil while whisking to create a smooth paste, adding water as needed to create a sauce-like consistency.

ASSEMBLY

Gently toss micro greens in a small amount of mustard sauce, salt, and pepper to lightly coat. Place crabs on a cutting board so the head is facing you. Cut directly down the middle of the crab splitting in two so each half has legs. Place one half on a serving plate and place 2-3 slices of chorizo chips and 2-3 slices of tomato chips on top of the crab. Divide the micro greens and place half on top of the chorizo and tomato. Add another layer of chorizo and tomato and the other half of the greens. Drizzle with a little more Chinese mustard sauce. Top with the other half of the crab and garnish with one slice of tomato chip. Drizzle serving plate with mustard sauce.

JACOB'S CREEK
RESERVE
Riesling
VINTAGE

fennel sandwich

with tuna tartar and rucola

YIELDS 1 PORTION

INGREDIENTS

½ oz. wild capers in sea salt

6 oz. tuna loin

1 oz. niçoise olive, pitted

1 oz. sun-dried tomatoes, chopped

1 tsp. chopped cilantro

Sea salt and black pepper, to taste

1 oz. oil laundemio

2 fennel bulbs

½ oz. wild rucola (arugula)

Olive oil, as needed

Lemon juice, as needed

METHOD

Rinse the capers in cold water. Chop the tuna, and mix with the capers, olives, sun-dried tomatoes, cilantro, salt, and olive oil. Slice the fennel, leaving the hard core attached so it does not fall apart.

ASSEMBLY

Compose the sandwich alternating the fennel, rucola, and tuna tartar. Repeat twice. Finish the dish with a dressing made of olive oil, lemon juice, salt and pepper.

Casa Tua

MIAMI BEACH

EXECUTIVE CHEF
Sergio Sigala

WYNDHAM ESTATE

BIN 222
CHARDONNAY

lobster blt

LOBSTER

6 oz. steamed lobster, rough chopped

1 Tbsp. celery, small dice

LOBSTER MAYONNAISE

1 egg yolk

1 Tbsp. celery root puree

1 Tbsp. lemon juice

½ tsp. lemon zest

2 Tbsp. lobster stock

1 cup canola oil

Salt and pepper, to taste

GARNISH

2 slices brioche

3 slices bacon

2 slices tomato

3 leaves Bibb lettuce

METHOD

Combine chopped lobster and celery in a mixing bowl. In a separate bowl, combine yolk, celery root, lemon juice, zest and stock. Slowly whisk in the oil until emulsified. Season with salt and pepper. Add the mayo in small increments to the lobster celery mixture until it is bound and creamy. Adjust seasoning with salt and pepper and spoon the mix onto freshly toasted brioche. Garnish with crisp warm bacon, tomato, and Bibb lettuce.

Citarella

EXECUTIVE CHEF
Jeremy Culver

purple haze goat cheese and black mission figs

YIELDS 1 PORTION

INGREDIENTS

2 oz. purple haze goat cheese

1 Tbsp. lavender honey

3 slices cranberry pecan bread, lightly toasted

15 leaves wild arugula

3 pieces black mission figs, quartered

METHOD

Mix the cheese and honey together to form a spread.

Spread the cheese mixture onto the slices of bread.

Top with the arugula and quartered figs.

CHARLIE PALMER'S

MÉTRAZUR

EXECUTIVE CHEF

Michael Lockard

saigon lobster roll

YIELDS 1 LOBSTER ROLL

INGREDIENTS

1 (1 ½ to 2 lb.) Maine lobster

1 sheet of rice paper (8 ½ inch diameter)

1 red bell pepper, finely julienned

1 green bell pepper, finely julienned

1 yellow bell pepper, finely julienned

1 small red onion, finely julienned

1 Tbsp. minced garlic

1 Tbsp. minced lemongrass

¼ bunch chopped cilantro

½ bunch basil, whole leaves and chiffonade

¼ to ½ daikon radish, finely julienned

BROTH FOR POACHING LOBSTER

2 stalks lemongrass

½ cup ginger, coarsely chopped

½ head garlic, coarsely chopped

2 bay leaves

1 gallon water

1 carrot, coarsely chopped

1 Spanish onion, coarsely chopped

2 stalks celery, coarsely chopped

1 Tbsp. whole black peppercorns

1 cup white wine

Salt, to taste

METHOD

Combine ingredients for broth and bring to a boil. Once at a rolling boil, add lobster. Cover for about 6-8 minutes. While cooking, prepare an ice bath to shock the lobster. Submerge the lobster in the ice bath, cool completely and begin removing the meat from the shell. Lightly crack the claws and reserve for the final presentation. Split the lobster tail down the middle and remove from the shell. Coarsely chop the tail meat and set aside.

MILLENNIUM
UN PLAZA HOTEL

NEW YORK

EXECUTIVE CHEF
Scott Owen

SOY MIRIN VINAIGRETTE

½ cup soy sauce

½ cup rice wine vinegar

Juice of 2-3 limes

¼ cup mirin

1 Tbsp. hoisin sauce

2 Tbsp. minced garlic

½ bunch scallions, chopped on bias

¼ cup sesame oil

Combine all of the ingredients, except the oil. Slowly whisk in the oil and reserve.

MANGO HABANERO HOT SAUCE

2 Tbsp. ginger, coarsely chopped

4 cloves garlic, coarsely chopped

2 habanero peppers, deseeded

2 shallots, coarsely chopped

Sweat the ginger, garlic, habaneros and shallots until they are soft, about 6 to 8 minutes. Add rice wine vinegar. Reduce by half. Add mango purée to pan and bring to a boil. Let simmer for about 5 minutes. Purée in a blender, slowly drizzling in the oil, until very smooth. Add the cumin and salt to taste.

CILANTRO MINT CHUTNEY

1 bunch cilantro

½ bunch mint

2 Tbsp. coarsely chopped ginger

Juice of 3 limes

4 garlic cloves

1 bunch scallions

Salt and pepper, to taste

½ cup corn oil

Place all ingredients in a blender, except the oil. Slowly drizzle in the oil and purée until smooth. Adjust seasoning, to taste.

1 cup rice wine vinegar

1 lb. mango puree

¼ cup corn oil

2 Tbsp. ground cumin

Salt, to taste

ASSEMBLY

Dip the rice paper in cool water for a few seconds until it starts to absorb the water. Lay flat on a cutting board. Cover with a damp towel. Take the chopped lobster meat, red onion, peppers, garlic, lemongrass, cilantro, basil and radish and toss with vinaigrette. Position the lobster mixture on the lower part of the rice paper. Roll it away from you. Tuck in the ends. Slice the roll on the bias. Pile extra vegetables in the center of the plate and put the cut lobster roll leaning against the vegetables. Place claws against the rolls and sauce the plate with the mango habanero sauce and chutney.

marinated white anchovies
soft boiled egg, frisée and roasted onion on country bread

YIELDS 1 SANDWICH

INGREDIENTS

1 soft boiled egg

2 ¹/₂-inch thick slices country bread

Salt and pepper, to taste

8 small filets white marinated anchovies,
   marinated in vinegar and olive oil, not salt
   cured, drained of excess oil on a paper towel

1 small handful frisée, white part only, dressed
   with Salsa Verde (recipe follows)

¹/₄ medium-large Spanish onion, sliced thinly and
   lightly caramelized

SALSA VERDE

(enough for 10 sandwiches)

1 bunch Italian parsley, chopped very fine

1 Tbsp. capers, chopped very fine

1 small garlic clove, minced

¹/₂ cup extra virgin olive oil

¹/₄ cup champagne vinegar

Kosher salt and freshly ground black pepper

METHOD

Cook the egg for 7 minutes in boiling water and shock in cold water. The white should be cooked through and the yolk should be runny. Once cold, the eggs can be peeled and held until serving. In a bowl, combine all of the chopped ingredients for the salsa verde. The sauce should be tangy and salty.

To compose the sandwich, slice the country bread about 1⁄2 inch thick and lightly toast one side. On the toasted side, slice one soft-boiled egg length-wise into about 6 pieces and spread, mashing it a little. Season with salt and pepper. Lay the anchovies over the egg, add the dressed frisée and top with a good amount of cold caramelized onion. Top with another slice of bread, slice in two and serve.

EXECUTIVE CHEF
Sisha Ortuzar

CHEF / OWNER
Tom Colicchio

grilled shrimp on pancetta club

INGREDIENTS

4 Tbsp. basil purée (recipe follows)

12 pieces of sliced brioche, toasted

4 slices of beefsteak tomato

4 pieces of Bibb lettuce

12 pieces cooked medium shrimp

4 pieces of cooked pancetta

SHRIMP

½ gallon water

2 Tbsp. kosher salt

1 stalk celery, sliced

1 onion, thinly sliced

2 bay leaves

1 Tbsp. whole white peppercorns

½ cup white wine

12 medium sized shrimp

BASIL PURÉE

1 bunch of basil

1 clove roasted garlic

½ cup olive oil

½ tsp. salt

Fresh black pepper, to taste

METHOD

Bring all of the ingredients, except the shrimp, to a boil. Add the shrimp and turn off the heat. Let stand for 15 minutes. Remove from the heat and let cool. Peel and butterfly.

METHOD

Blanch and shock the basil. Place the basil and garlic in the blender and slowly add the oil. Season with 1/2 tsp. salt and a few grinds of the pepper mill.

ASSEMBLY

Use the basil purée as butter and coat the toasted bread. The first layer is the tomato and the lettuce. Add the cooked butterfly shrimp and the warm pancetta. Top with the remaining slice of bread. Use bamboo skewers and cut each in four pieces.

EXECUTIVE CHEF
Patricia Williams

fishing fa frank burger

INGREDIENTS

4 oz. whiting

Salt and pepper, to taste

Flour, as needed (for breading)

1 egg, beaten

Cornmeal, as needed (for breading)

Vegetable oil, as needed (for frying)

Mayonnaise, to taste

Hard roll

1 beef frank, cooked, cut in half
    lengthwise

1 onion, sliced thin and sautéed

Baby spinach, as needed

Crushed red pepper, to taste

METHOD

Season the fish with salt and pepper. Dust the fish with flour, then dip in the egg and finally in the cornmeal. Pour enough oil into a skillet to come halfway up the fish. Heat the oil and add the fish. As soon as the first side is browned, flip and brown the other side. Remove to paper towels.

ASSEMBLY

Spread some mayonnaise on a hard roll. Place the fish, then the beef frank, the onion and spinach on the roll. Season with some crushed red pepper.

THE CHILDREN'S STOREFRONT
An Independent School in Harlem

CHEF
Stephen Alleyne

the trumpwich

SERVES 1

INGREDIENTS

6 oz. lean corned beef, sliced thin

2 oz. fresh roasted turkey breast

2 oz. imported Swiss cheese

2 oz. deli style cole slaw

2 slices fresh pumpernickel bread

CONDIMENTS

Silken tofu

Spicy mustard

Russian dressing

Dill pickles and olives

METHOD

Place pumpernickel on cutting board and place items according to recipe, slice in half.

EXECUTIVE CHEF

Christopher Devine

strawberry panino

with aceto balsamico

YIELDS 2 SERVINGS

INGREDIENTS

3 slices Italian sponge cake, ½ inch thick
   (recipe follows)

2 cups strawberry gelato (recipe follows)

1 Tbsp. unsalted butter

2 Tbsp. extra virgin olive oil

1 cup sliced, fresh strawberries, tossed

2 tsp. granulated sugar

2 tsp. aceto balsamico tradizionale,
   18 or 25 year (vecchio or stravecchio)

Confectioner's sugar, as needed (for dusting)

Make the sponge cake and strawberry gelato 1 or 2 days in advance of assembling the panini.

RISTORANTE
BABBO
ENOTECA

CHEF / OWNER
Mario Batali

PASTRY CHEF
Gina DePalma

ITALIAN SPONGE CAKE (PAN DI SPAGNA)

1 cup sifted cake flour

½ tsp. baking powder

½ tsp. kosher salt

4 large eggs, separated

¾ cup granulated sugar

1 tsp. pure vanilla extract

Grated zest of 1 lemon

½ cup (1 stick) unsalted butter,
   melted and cooled

A pinch of kosher salt

¼ tsp. cream of tartar

METHOD

Preheat the oven to 350°. Grease and flour a 9 inch loaf pan. Sift together the cake flour, baking powder and salt into a medium bowl and set aside. In the bowl of an electric mixer fitted with the whisk attachment, beat the egg yolks together with the sugar on medium speed until very light, pale yellow in color, and doubled in volume, about 3 minutes. Beat in the vanilla extract and lemon zest, followed by the melted butter. Transfer the egg mixture to a large, clean mixing bowl. Fold in the dry ingredients quickly and lightly, using a rubber spatula, stopping just before they are fully incorporated. Clean the whisk attachment and mixing bowl to prepare them for whipping the egg whites. Place the egg whites and a pinch of salt in the cleaned bowl of the electric mixer. Using the whip attachment on medium-high speed, beat the egg whites until they are foamy and light. Add the cream of tartar, and continue beating until stiff peaks form. Fold the egg whites into the batter quickly and lightly. This will also incorporate any streaks of dry ingredients that remained. Spoon the batter into the prepared pan, filling it 3/4 full and smoothing the tops. Bake the cake for 35 to 45 minutes, or until a cake tester inserted in the center comes out clean and the cake has begun to pull away from the sides of the pan.

recipe continues on page 186

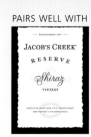

hot & cold cheese steak

raw prime rib sandwich

INGREDIENTS

1 medium red onion, thinly sliced

Salt and pepper, to taste

4 slices firm old world style
pumpernickel (round preferred)

12 oz. very rare roast beef (prime rib
preferably), thinly sliced

4 oz. pecorino cheese with black truffle,
thinly sliced (any good hard Italian
cheese can be substituted)

5 Tbsp. extra virgin olive oil

METHOD

Toss the onion with the 1 Tbsp. olive oil, salt, and pepper. Place 4 rounds of pumpernickel bread out on surface. Drape 3 oz. of sliced beef in middle on bread. Season with salt and pepper. Place 1/4 of the shaved dressed red onion slices on top of beef. Layer 1 oz. of sliced cheese on top of each. Drizzle with 1 Tbsp. extra virgin olive oil on each sandwich.

The Institute
of Culinary Education

EXECUTIVE CHEF
Andrew Gold

grilled wagyu sirloin

INGREDIENTS

12 cipollini onions, peeled

¼ cup balsamic vinegar

2 Tbsp. sugar

Salt and pepper, to taste

8 pieces sliced onion bread, toasted
in frying pan in 3 Tbsp. butter,
kept warm

12 oz. grilled sirloin steak, thinly sliced

4 oz. Cotswold cheddar or any good
sharp cheddar cheese, thinly sliced

METHOD

Toss the onions with the balsamic vinegar, sugar, salt, and pepper and roast at 275° for two hours, tossing regularly until browned and tender. Preheat an oven to 300°. Place 4 slices of pan-toasted onion bread on metal tray. Layer 3 oz. of sliced grilled steak on each slice of bread. Cut the roasted cipollini onions in half from the top side to the root end. Place 6 pieces on each sandwich. Layer 1 oz. of sliced cheese on each sandwich. Top with the second piece of toasted bread. Place in the oven about 4-5 minutes until cheese slightly melted. Remove and serve.

GAUFRETTE POTATO CHIPS

1 lb. starchy potatoes (colored fingerlings
preferred) peeled and sliced on
mandoline and placed in water.

2 cups grape seed or clear vegetable oil

Maldon sea salt, to taste

METHOD

In a shallow sauce pot, heat the oil to 275°. Dry the potato slices thoroughly. Place potatoes in the oil and cook stirring occasionally until the chips come out crisp and are slightly browned on the edges. Dry on towel. Sprinkle with Maldon sea salt or your favorite natural salt flakes.

ASSEMBLY

Place 1 of each sandwich on a large plate. Place a small pile of potato chips towards the front of the sandwiches. Garnish with cornichons (pickles) and tomato wedges.

ciabatta sandwich

YIELDS 2 SANDWICHES

INGREDIENTS

1 3" x 5" ciabatta roll or bread
   (or use a whole loaf and cut)

Olive oil, as needed

1 oz. sliced Genoa salami

2 oz. sliced Black Forest ham

2 slices provolone cheese

2 Tbsp. Parmesan mayo (recipe follows)

2 leaves fresh basil

1 leaf of lettuce

2 slices fresh tomato

PARMESAN MAYO

½ cup mayonnaise

2 Tbsp. grated Parmesan

METHOD

Combine mayonnaise and Parmesan cheese. *Parmesan mayo goes well with many sandwiches, so you might consider making a batch to keep in the refrigerator. It will keep for up to 30 days.*

Preheat oven to 350°. Cut roll crosswise and place open-faced on a baking sheet. Spread top piece of bread with olive oil. On the bottom piece, place salami, ham, and provolone cheese. Build a second sandwich the same way. Place pan with sandwiches in the oven and bake for about 10 minutes. When done, the bread should be toasted and the cheese melted. Remove sandwiches from the oven. Spread Parmesan mayo evenly over the toasted bread. Place basil, lettuce and tomato on top of melted cheese. Close sandwich and cut in half on the diagonal to serve.

COOK TIME TurboChef oven: 1 minute, 15 seconds
                     Conventional oven: 10 to 15 minutes

EXECUTIVE CHEF
Alison Brushaber

roasted vegetable & mozzarella sandwich

INGREDIENTS

1 Roma tomato

Extra virgin olive oil, as needed

1 clove garlic

1 sprig fresh thyme, chopped

Salt and black pepper, to taste

1 Japanese eggplant

1 zucchini

1 oz. Brocconcini mozzarella

1 Robuchon's finger baguette

1 sprig fresh basil

METHOD

Cut tomato into 6 pieces and de-seed. Place on a tray and drizzle with olive oil. Slice garlic thinly. Place one slice of garlic and some fresh thyme on each tomato slice. Season with salt and pepper and cook slowly in a 200° oven for one hour. Turn tomatoes halfway through. While tomatoes are cooking, cut eggplant and zucchini on a bias, 1/2 inch thick. Season each side with salt and pepper. Heat a sauté pan and add extra virgin olive oil. Sauté vegetables until each side has a nice color. Let vegetables cool. Slice mozzarella 1/2 inch thick. Cut the bread in half. Place the eggplant, mozzarella, zucchini and Roma tomato slices accordingly. Decorate with fresh basil tops.

L'ATELIER de Joël Robuchon

FOUNDING CHEF
Jöel Robuchon

EXECUTIVE CHEF
Yosuke Suga

alsatian pastrami & foie gras sandwich

PASTRAMI

1 lb. beef brisket

1 Tbsp. salt

1 tsp. whole black pepper

1 tsp. coriander seeds

½ tsp. mustard seeds

1 bay leaf

1 clove garlic, roughly chopped

1 carrot, roughly chopped

1 medium onion, roughly chopped

1 celery stalk, roughly chopped

POTATOES

2 oz. fingerling potatoes

1 clove garlic

1 sprig rosemary

Salt, to taste

1 piece shallot

1 sprig fresh thyme, chopped

1 tsp. sherry vinegar

Extra virgin olive oil, as needed

1 oz. foie gras terrine

Radishes, as needed

Chives, as needed

1 Robuchon's small campagne bread

METHOD

Combine all of the ingredients for the pastrami in a large pot and cover with water. Cook on low heat for 4 to 5 hours. Let it cool. Slice the brisket very thinly.

In another pot, combine fingerling potatoes, garlic, and rosemary. Cover with water. Add salt to the water and cook until potatoes are cooked. Chop the shallot, peel the potatoes, cut 1/4 inch thick. Sprinkle with thyme and sherry vinegar and cover with olive oil. Let it rest.

Slice cold foie gras terrine very thinly. Make curls with your hand. Refrigerate.

Thinly slice and cut the radishes into sticks. Cut chives the same size as radishes.

Slice bread in half. Place meat slices, foie gras terrine slices and potato slices accordingly. Decorate with radishes and chives.

chicken pot pie (remix)

SANDWICHES of the WORLD

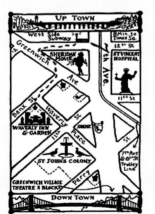

THE WAVERLY INN & GARDEN

EXECUTIVE CHEF	SOUS CHEF	SOUS CHEF
John DeLucie	Nick Cataldo	Domingo Gabriel

INGREDIENTS

3 chicken breasts

6 chicken thighs

1 medium onion, diced

2 stalks celery, sliced

3 whole carrots, chopped

1 cup baby carrots, chopped, blanched
    and shocked in ice water

Salt and pepper, to taste

1 cup frozen green peas, blanched and
    shocked in ice water

1 cup cremini mushrooms, quartered,
    sautéed in butter, and cooled

½ cup pearl onions (fresh or frozen) peeled,
    blanched and shocked in ice water

1 sheet frozen puff pastry

1 whole egg beaten

1 recipe chicken sauce (recipe follows)

CHICKEN SAUCE

3 Tbsp. butter

3 Tbsp. all-purpose flour

¼ cup chicken broth

½ cup heavy cream

½ tsp. Worcestershire sauce, to taste

½ tsp. Tabasco, to taste

Salt and pepper, to taste

METHOD

Preheat oven to 425°. Place chicken, onion, celery, whole carrots, salt, and pepper in large stock pot and cover with water. Simmer in covered pot until chicken is no longer pink, approximately 25 minutes. Strain the broth and set aside to use in the chicken cream sauce. Remove chicken and cool.

Cut chicken into bite size pieces. In a non-reactive bowl, combine the celery, chopped baby carrots, peas, mushrooms, onions, and chicken. Evenly divide mixture into four-6-inch pie pans. Cut puff pastry to fit pie pan, leaving a 2 inch border. Lay puff pastry over filling and crimp edges, trimming edges if necessary. Cut a hole in the center of the pastry to allow steam to escape. Beat 1 whole egg and brush over crust. Bake until crust is golden brown and filling is bubbly, approximately 25 minutes. Let stand 5 minutes before serving.

METHOD

Melt the butter in a medium saucepan and then stir in the flour. Add the reserved chicken broth and heavy cream. Stir constantly until mixture comes to a boil. Reduce heat and simmer for two minutes. Remove from heat, add Worcestershire, Tabasco, salt and pepper.

thai market crêpe

BATTER

1 cup rice flour

¼ cup tapioca flour

¼ cup glutinous rice flour

½ tsp. turmeric powder

1 egg

1 tsp. salt

1 cup coconut milk

1 cup water

FILLING

¼ cup vegetable oil

1 tsp. chopped garlic

1 tsp. chopped cilantro

1 tsp. white pepper

2 tsp. shrimp oil

1 cup chopped shrimp

1 tsp. ground, salted turnip

1 ½ Tbsp. fish sauce

¼ cup palm sugar

1 cup coconut flakes

1 ½ cups bean sprouts

METHOD

Mix the three flours together. Add the turmeric, egg, and salt. Slowly stir in coconut milk and water until a thick, smooth consistency is achieved.

Heat a frying pan and add the vegetable oil. Add garlic, cilantro, pepper, and sauté. Add shrimp oil, shrimp, and turnip and cook until shrimp is done. Add fish sauce, palm sugar and coconut flakes. Sauté briefly and set aside.

Heat a pan on low with vegetable oil until hot. Pour the batter into the pan, making sure the mixture is evenly distributed. Wait until the crepe is crispy and toss in the stir-fry ingredients and fresh bean sprouts. Fold the crepe in half.

T H A I market

EXECUTIVE CHEF
Tanaporn Tangwibulchai

db burger royale

Don't try this one at home kids! Keep in mind that the DB Burger is actually two dishes in one: outside a seemingly traditional ground sirloin hamburger, and inside a taste of France. Daniel Boulud loves burgers and considers them an essential part of the American culinary tradition. His DB Burger is a tribute to that and is his way of combining the best of France and America in one dish.

The classic French dish "Tournedos Rossini" inspires the DB Burger's filling. A roasted tournedo served with a foie gras and a black truffle sauce. For the burger, we begin by braising short ribs in red wine, a day-long labor of love in and of itself. Once removed from the bone, the meat is combined with a mirepoix of root vegetables and preserved black truffle. The mixture is then carefully molded around a center of tender seared foie gras. Finally, the luxurious stuffing is enveloped in a layer of ground sirloin and is ready for searing.

To finish this ultimate sandwich, a homemade toasted Parmesan and poppy seed bun is layered with a touch of fresh horseradish, oven roasted tomato confit, fresh tomato, frisée lettuce and red onion. Pair the burger with a side of pomme soufflées et voila!

db
bistro moderne

EXECUTIVE CHEF
Daniel Boulud

caramelized duck legs

SERVES 4

INGREDIENTS

Kosher salt and fresh ground pepper, to taste

2 duck legs

Extra virgin olive oil, as needed

2 Tbsp. butter, softened

4 heads Belgium endive, thinly sliced crosswise

1 Tbsp. sugar

5 sprigs thyme leaves

1 loaf sliced country bread, each slice cut into
    a rectangle (crust removed)

½ cup orange marmalade

1 small Burgundy truffle, thinly sliced

METHOD

Generously salt and pepper the duck legs. Over medium heat, warm the olive oil in a frying pan. Add the duck legs and cover with a lid. Watch closely until the skin is crisp and the meat is cooked through. Allow them to cool.

In a separate pan over high heat, add 1 Tbsp. olive oil and 1 Tbsp. butter and cook until it begins to foam. Add sliced endive, sugar, salt, thyme, and pepper to taste. Cook until caramelized. Remove from heat and cover to keep warm.

Pick the meat from the legs and reserve the skin (for garnish) and some of the fat in the pan. Fold the duck meat into endive. With a pastry brush, brush each slice of bread with duck fat on one side. Season with salt and pepper, then toast each in a toaster until golden brown. Spread the orange marmalade onto the toasts from edge to edge. Place a layer of the duck and endive mixture on top. Garnish with sliced truffles and duck skin. Serve with mixed greens or raw endive salad*.

The endive salad can be composed of sliced endive, strips of candied orange zest and pickled mustard seeds.

craft

EXECUTIVE CHEF
Damon Wise

CHEF / OWNER
Tom Colicchio

rainbow steamed fish

INGREDIENTS

12 turnips, sliced thin, 3 x 1½

12 carrots, sliced thin, 3 x 1½

12 leeks, sliced thin, 3 x 1½

8 pieces of sea bass, 3 x 1½

Salt and white pepper, to taste

4 whole dry mushrooms,
    cut into a fan shape

1 Tbsp. chicken stock

½ Tbsp. Shaoxing rice wine

1 tsp. sesame oil

METHOD

Divide the turnip, carrot, leeks and sea bass into thirds. Season with salt and pepper. Layer first third of turnips, carrots, leeks and sea bass. Repeat two more times to make 3 layers and then top with mushroom fan.

Sprinkle the chicken stock and rice wine on top, season, and drizzle the sesame oil around the plate. Steam for 8 minutes and serve.

EXECUTIVE CHEF
Cheng-Hua Yang

ASSEMBLED BY PASTRY CHEF
Nicholas Lee

summer pancetta & heirloom tomato sandwich

SERVES 4

INGREDIENTS

½ cup burrata cheese

1 Tbsp. lemon zest

2 Tbsp. chopped basil

¼ cup extra virgin olive oil,
   plus extra as needed

Sea salt and fresh ground
   black pepper, to taste

¼ cup toy box tomatoes

8 slices pancetta, thinly sliced

4 each herb focaccia bread
   (4"x 6" rectangles)

½ cup cannellini bean purée

½ cup arugula

8 slices assorted heirloom
   tomato, thinly sliced

¼ cup sliced French radishes

METHOD

Shred the soft burrata cheese by hand, pulling it lightly apart. Place the cheese in a bowl and mix lightly with the lemon zest, chopped basil, 1/4 cup olive oil, sea salt, and freshly ground black pepper and marinate for 10 minutes. Cut a few toy box tomatoes into quarters. Cook the pancetta on the griddle until crisp. Pat dry with a cloth or paper towels to remove any excess oil.

Cut the herb focaccia bread lengthwise to create top and bottom sandwich layers. Brush the cut side of each slice of focaccia bread with olive oil and lightly grill in a pan or on a griddle until golden brown. Spread a healthy dollop of cannelloni bean purée on the bottom layer of focaccia bread. Layer the top with fresh arugula lettuce followed by 2 slices of heirloom tomatoes. Season the tomato layer with extra virgin olive oil, sea salt, and freshly ground black pepper. Place a slice of the crisped pancetta on top of the tomato.

Layer on the shredded burrata cheese and toy box tomato quarters and the top slice of the herb focaccia bread. Place the sandwich on a plate and garnish with thin slices of French radish. Serve immediately so the sandwich ingredients remain crisp and to preserve the fresh flavors.

NOTE FROM THE CHEF

A wonderful and suggested side dish for this sandwich is roasted sweet potato wedges.

MANDARIN ORIENTAL

NEW YORK

SM

EXECUTIVE CHEF
Toni Robertson

smoked salmon pizzette

SERVES 4

INGREDIENTS

20 slices smoked Atlantic salmon

½ cup crème fraiche

3 Tbsp. Gold's prepared horseradish

Salt and freshly ground black pepper

½ small red onion, peeled and thinly sliced

2 sprigs fresh dill, picked

2 sprigs fresh tarragon, picked

4 fresh large pita breads

20 small capers

½ oz. caviar

METHOD

In a large bowl, whisk the crème fraiche until soft peaks form. Add horse-radish, salt and pepper. Let stand to chill at least 1 hour in advance. Over a hot, seasoned grill, lightly toast the pita breads, turning to brown evenly. Remove from heat and transfer to a plate to cool to room temperature. Divide the crème fraiche mixture evenly among the pita breads. Spread with an icing spatula to coat the pitas. Carefully arrange the smoked salmon slices to cover the entire pita evenly. Sprinkle the picked herbs all over the smoked salmon. Drape with the sliced red onions. Cut into even wedges and garnish with capers and caviar.

EXECUTIVE CHEF
Geoffrey Zakarian

grilled white cheddar, bacon and leek sandwich

56

SERVES 4

INGREDIENTS

1 lb. Grafton Village Extra Aged White Cheddar,
    or other extra sharp white cheddar

12 strips Niman Ranch applewood smoked bacon,
    or other applewood smoked bacon

2 large leeks

2 Tbsp. olive oil

Salt and peppe,r to taste

8 slices Pain D'Avignon 7 Grain Pullman,
    Whole Foods organic 12 grain bread,
    or other multi-grain bread

8 tsp. chipotle mustard (recipe follows)

8 tsp. unsalted butter

CHIPOTLE MUSTARD

½ cup Grey Poupon or other Dijon style mustard

6 Tbsp. light brown sugar

4 Tbsp. chipotle purée

METHOD

Shred cheese on the coarse side of a hand grater, and reserve. Lay bacon flat in a single layer on a large baking sheet and bake for 13-15 minutes at 350°, or to desired crispness. Cut each slice in half. Reserve.

Trim dark green outer leaves from leeks, then cut in half lengthwise and rinse carefully, to remove any soil. Season leeks with olive oil, salt and pepper, then grill or broil until cooked through. Thinly slice and reserve. (Leeks may also be thinly sliced, then sautéed in olive oil until soft and just beginning to turn golden).

To make the chipotle mustard, purée 1 can chipotle chiles en adobo (available in most supermarkets) in blender until smooth, adding a little water to release blades if necessary. Combine with Dijon style mustard and brown sugar and mix well.

METHOD

If using Pain D'Avignon or other unsliced bread, cut eight 3/8 inch slices. Spread each slice of bread with 1 tsp. chipotle mustard. Top each of 4 slices with 2 oz. (1/2 cup) grated cheese, 3 half slices of bacon, a quarter of the leeks, 3 more half slices bacon, 2 oz. cheese, and a second slice of bread. Butter the outside of each sandwich and cook on griddle or in a large frying pan until golden brown on one side. Turn and continue cooking until golden brown on second side.

EXECUTIVE CHEF
Jan Mendelson

soft shell crab on brioche

YIELDS 4 SANDWICHES

INGREDIENTS

Tartar sauce, as needed

8 slices of brioche

8 pieces baby fennel (recipe follows)

8 cherry tomatoes (recipe follows)

2 large artichokes (recipe follows)

20 ramps (recipe follows)

4 live soft shell crabs (recipe follows)

Olive oil, as needed (for tomatoes)

Salt and pepper, to taste

Bowl of ice water (for fennel)

BABY FENNEL

Bring a medium sized pot of water to a boil with a pinch of salt. Set aside a bowl of ice water. Place the fennel in the boiling water and cook for about 2 minutes, or until tender. Remove from pot and place in the ice water to cool.

CHERRY TOMATOES

Slice the tomatoes in half. Drizzle with olive oil, and season with salt and pepper. Place on a very hot grill, sliced side down and sear for about 30 seconds, or long enough to slightly char the flesh.

ARTICHOKES

2 large artichokes

Salt and pepper, to taste

2 Tbsp. plus 1 cup olive oil

¼ tsp. fennel seed

½ cup cider vinegar

1 Tbsp. salt

½ Tbsp. sugar

¼ tsp. herbs de Provence
   (rosemary, marjoram, basil,
   thyme, bay leaf, lavender)

¼ tsp. mustard seed

¼ tsp. coriander seed

¼ tsp. black pepper

1 bay leaf

RAMPS

Salt, as needed

4 slices of bacon

CRAB

Salt and pepper, to taste

2 Tbsp. olive oil

1 Tbsp. butter

1 clove garlic

2 sprigs thyme

METHOD

Peel the artichokes and empty out the chokes. Cut in half, season well with salt and pepper, and place in a medium sauté pan with 2 Tbsp. olive oil and fennel seeds. Cook artichokes on medium-low heat, stirring occasionally, making sure not to brown, for about 10-15 minutes or until tender. Combine with the rest of the ingredients and let marinate in the refrigerator until ready to use.

Bring a small pot of water to a boil with a pinch of salt. While holding ramps in bundles of five, grip the stems and dip bulbs into boiling water for about ten seconds. Wrap bulbs of each bundle in one slice of bacon. Wrap leaves in a small piece of aluminum foil. Sear bulbs on all sides in a medium sized sauté pan over medium heat until bacon begins to crisp. Remove from pan and remove foil from the leaves.

Clean crabs with a sharp pair of scissors by lifting the top shell on both sides and cutting away the lungs. Turn crab upside down, lift the flap between the legs, and cut away the apron. Cut away the head of the crab (eyes and mouth). Season both sides well with salt and pepper. Heat a medium sized sauté pan to medium-high with olive oil and butter. Place in the hot pan and sear, while basting, for about 2 minutes on each side, adding 1 garlic clove and thyme halfway through cooking.

ASSEMBLY

Spread a spoonful of tartar sauce on each slice of bread. Top one slice with fennel, cherry tomatoes, artichokes, ramp bundle and warm crab. Top with another slice of brioche.

NEW YORK • PALM BEACH

EXECUTIVE CHEF

Bertrand Chemel

grilled bluefin tuna burger

INGREDIENTS

4½ lbs. ground tuna
½ cup shallots, minced
½ cup ginger, peeled
 and minced
¼ tsp. red thai chili,
 minced
½ tsp. sesame oil

METHOD

Clean sinew from tuna and grind with a large die into a hotel pan on ice. Carefully spread tuna to cover entire hotel pan. Sprinkle the surface with remaining ingredients and mix carefully. Form into 7 oz. patties without working the meat.

BONITO MAYONNAISE

½ cup, plus ¼ cup bonito flakes
¾ cup water
2 egg yolks
1 tsp. salt
2½ Tbsp. yuzu juice
2 cups grape seed oil

METHOD

Put 1/2 cup bonito flakes in a quart container. Bring water to a boil and immediately pour over bonito. Let steep 8 minutes, then strain, pushing hard for total extraction. Put 3 Tbsp. of the bonito broth into the robo coup with yolks, salt and yuzu and process. Emulsify with the oil. Add the remaining bonito flakes and pulse quickly. Reserve refrigerated until needed.

PICKLES

4 cups cucumber, washed and
 channeled with a peeler, sliced
 full opening on a mandoline
4 cups Japanese rice vinegar
¾ cup yuzu juice
1½ cups sugar
1 Tbsp. salt
2 Thai chilis, washed and split

METHOD

Put cucumbers in a baine. Combine vinegar, sugar, chilis, and salt and bring to a boil. Do not let roll. Add yuzu juice and cool over ice. Pour over pickles 4 hours prior to use.

BONITO POTATO CHIPS

METHOD

Slice Idaho potatoes thin on mandoline and rinse in water until all starch is gone. Fry potatoes at 300° until crispy and season thoroughly with bonito salt (grind equal parts bonito flakes and salt until fine).

PRESENTATION

Season with salt and white pepper, brush with light soy sauce and olive oil and grill on high until medium rare. Cut a Kaiser roll in half and brush with olive oil. Grill until toasted and warm. Apply bonito mayonnaise to both sides of the bun. Lay burger on the bottom bun. Place two big leaves of Boston lettuce, two shiso leaves and about 10 slices of pickles. Place top bun, secure burger with two bamboo picks and cut in half with electric knife. Serve with a side of potato chips.

SANDWICHES of the WORLD

PerrySt

CHEF / OWNER
Jean-Georges Vongerichten

STONELEIGH
—MARLBOROUGH—
RIESLING
WINE OF NEW ZEALAND

pickled beef tongue
with fried mayonnaise

requires advance preparation

TONGUE

1 (2-3 lb.) calf tongue
½ cup chopped celery
½ cup chopped onion
½ cup chopped carrot
2 cloves garlic, chopped
1 Tbsp. butter
1 Tbsp. grated ginger
5 pieces allspice
9 Tbsp. brown sugar
1 cup rice vinegar
2 cups chicken stock
1½ tsp. salt

METHOD

Soak the tongue in cold water for one day, changing the water frequently. Cook the celery, onion, carrot, and garlic in butter over medium heat for five minutes. Add the tongue and the remaining ingredients, bring to a simmer, and cook for 4-5 hours or until tender. Allow to cool in liquid. Peel off skin and trim away any fat. Slice tongue lengthwise on a meat slicer, on number 5.

TOMATO MOLASSES

14 oz. tomato
3½ oz. butter
3½ oz. molasses
Salt, to taste
Tabasco sauce, to taste

METHOD

Peel and seed the tomatoes and roughly chop. Warm the butter and molasses together, add tomatoes and cook down slowly until mixture thickens (about 6-8 hours). Allow to cool. Season with salt and Tabasco, blend to a smooth paste.

wd~50

CHEF / OWNER
Wylie Dufresne

FRIED MAYONNAISE

⅔ tsp. gellan
8 oz. cold milk
16 oz. grapeseed oil
1 tsp. gelatin
2 Tbsp. mustard
1 Tbsp. lemon juice
1½ Tbsp. salt
¼ tsp. pepper
½ cup flour
1 egg
1 egg yolk
½ cup panko breadcrumbs

METHOD

Shear the gellan into the cold milk. Bring to a boil and cook, stirring constantly, until the gellan is fully hydrated (you will be able to tell from the texture. When gellan gum is heated to 122°, it swells rapidly to form a thick, pasty suspension. At approximately 194° the suspension loses viscosity suddenly, signifying complete hydration). Heat the oil to 210°. Dissolve the gelatin in cold water. Dissolve the gelatin/water mixture into the hot milk mixture and slowly whisk in the hot oil, being careful to add only a little at a time. Once the oil has been incorporated, heat the mustard, lemon juice, salt, and pepper, and fold into the mixture. Spread onto a half sheet pan and cool. Once cool, cut into cubes and coat with flour, egg and panko breadcrumbs. Deep fry at 350°, until golden.

RED ONION STREUSEL

4 oz. butter
2½ oz. red onion powder
2 oz. flour
3½ oz. almond flour
1¾ tsp. salt

METHOD

Allow butter to soften. Mix all of the ingredients together and bake on a flat sheet tray at 300° for 10 minutes. Wrap the streusel tightly in plastic to maintain freshness. The texture should be crumbly.

PRESENTATION

Olive oil, as needed
Balinese salt crystals, to taste
Lettuce, chiffonade, as needed

METHOD

Warm the mayonnaise in oven for 2-3 minutes. Drizzle some olive oil on the sliced tongue and top with salt crystals. Place some tomato molasses on plate around the tongue. Decorate with red onion streusel and chiffonade of lettuce.

duck breast toscano

YIELDS 1 SANDWICH

INGREDIENTS

1 medium-sized duck breast

1 tsp. black pepper

2 tsp. salt

1 tsp. sugar

½ tsp. ground cloves

3 sprigs rosemary, roughly chopped

3 sprigs sage, roughly chopped

3 slices of Tuscan bread,
   (preferably day old)

Extra virgin olive oil, as needed

1-2 garlic cloves

2 Tbsp. mustard

4-6 slices of fontina cheese

1 small onion, sliced and put in vinegar

METHOD

Marinate the duck breast with black pepper, salt, sugar, cloves, and herbs overnight. Trim the duck breast fat to leave about 2/3 of the fat intact and then score the rest in order to render the fat during cooking. In a preheated 300° oven, cook the duck breast skin-side down until the fat is well rendered. Turn and continue turning every 10 minutes until an internal temperature of 140° is reached. Remove from pan and let cool.

Toast the bread with extra virgin olive oil and rub with garlic. Place the mustard, fontina cheese and onion on all pieces of toast. Slice the duck breast thin using a deli slicer, then place the duck on two of the three slices of bread (one slice is reserved for the middle of the sandwich.) Take the third piece and place atop one of the slices of bread. Take the remaining piece and put it on top to finish the sandwich. Place the sandwich into an oven to melt the cheese and heat the duck. Remove the toasted sandwich from the oven, slice and serve.

BEPPE

EXECUTIVE CHEF
Marc Taxiera

SOUS CHEF
March Walker

bo sam

INGREDIENTS

2 cups short grain rice

6 cups water

1 lb. beef rib eye, thinly sliced

1 head Boston lettuce

1 white onion, sliced

2 oz. Korean red miso paste

MARINADE

¼ green apple

¼ Asian pear

2 Tbsp. light soy sauce

2 Tbsp. sesame oil

½ tsp. black pepper

1 tsp. garlic, minced

METHOD

Wash the rice in cold water, drain and add 6 cups water to a pot or rice cooker. If using a pot, bring water to a boil, then reduce heat to medium, cover and cook for approximately 20-25 minutes. Add more water if necessary.

For the marinade, puree 1/4 apple and 1/4 pear together in a food processor or blender until finely ground. Drain excess liquid. In a large bowl combine all the marinade ingredients and the meat and gently mix, making sure not to tear the meat excessively. Meanwhile, cut the bottom off the Boston lettuce, carefully separate the leaves and wash them individually in cold water. Drain and refrigerate.

In a large sauté pan over high heat, sauté the marinated meat and sliced onion for approximately 5-7 minutes or until cooked to preferred doneness. It is recommended to cook the meat in 2-3 batches.

ASSEMBLY

To assemble, place a spoonful of rice onto the center of a leaf of lettuce. Add a small amount of miso paste and spread over rice. Add a few slices of meat and onion on top of the rice and gently bring both sides of lettuce together.

Woo Lae Oak

EXECUTIVE CHEF
Harold Soo Hyung Kim

toasted organic egg yolk

with caviar and dill

INGREDIENTS

4 eggs, room temperature

8 thick slices brioche (3 inch long,
 1 ½ inch wide, ¼ inch thick

1 Tbsp. butter, room temperature

Salt and white pepper, to taste

METHOD

Using a thermal circulator, bring a water bath to 148°. Cook the eggs for 1 hour, then cool in an ice bath. Separate the yolk from the white, removing any traces of white from the yolk. Spread a thin layer of butter on each piece of bread. Cut each yolk in half, laying cut side up on the bread. Season well with salt and pepper. Top with another piece of brioche, forming a sandwich. Set Plancha to level 5 and add a pat of butter. Sauté the toasts until golden on both sides. Blot them on paper towel.

GARNISH

Fleur de Sel

Caviar

Dill pluche

ASSEMBLY

Top each egg toast with a quenelle of caviar, a few grains of Fleur de Sel and dill pluche.

SANDWICHES of the WORLD

CHEF DE CUISINE

Greg Brainin

JACOB'S CREEK®

RIESLING

VINTAGE

blackened blue fish blt
with spinach salad

SERVES 1

INGREDIENTS

Vegetable oil, as needed

5 oz. blue fish, skin left on

2 tsp. Cajun spices

1 Pepper roll toasted

Lemon mayonnaise

2 slices ripe tomato

2 pieces thick bacon

1 piece romaine lettuce

LEMON MAYONNAISE

1/4 cup Hellmann's mayonnaise

1 tsp. Dijon mustard

Few drops lemon juice

SPINACH SALAD

Baby spinach, as desired

Red onion, as desired

Walnuts, toasted, as desired

Blue cheese dressing, as desired

METHOD

Heat up a cast iron skillet or frying pan until very hot. Drizzle with vegetable oil. Pat the fish with the Cajun spices on the skin side. Sear for 2 minutes. Turn over and cook for 1-2 minutes on the second side, or until fish is done. Assemble the sandwich with the remaining ingredients. Serve with spinach salad.

Combine ingredients and mix well.

Conbine ingredients and toss.

good enough to eat

CHEF / OWNER

Carrie Levin

grilled cheese soup
with tomato "sandwiches"

GRILLED CHEESE SOUP

7 small onions, sliced

5 carrots, peeled and diced

5 cloves of garlic, sliced

1 fresh jalapeño, seeded and sliced

Grapeseed oil, as needed

2 Tbsp. baking soda

4 Heinekens (3 for the soup and
    one for the cook!)

2 qts. chicken stock

1½ lbs. cheddar cheese, grated

2 drops Worcestershire sauce

¼ lb Parmesan cheese

METHOD

On low heat, slowly sweat out the vegetables in a little bit of grapeseed oil. Add the baking soda and beer, reduce by half and add the chicken stock. Slowly add the cheese while blending the ingredients in a blender. Strain and add the Worcestershire sauce.

Grate 1/4 lb. of Parmesan cheese. In a non-stick pan, make small piles of the grated cheese, each the size of a silver dollar, and bake for ten minutes or until golden brown. Remove and reserve.

TOMATO SANDWICHES

3 medium sized vine ripened tomatoes

Salt and pepper, to taste

Olive oil, as needed

4 large slices brioche

2 oz. fresh thyme

METHOD

Dust the tomatoes with salt, pepper and olive oil and allow them to marinate. Place toasted brioche in food processor and grind.

For the presentation, simply alternate tomatoes and Parmesan crisps in a circle garnished with the herbs and your ground toast. Pour the soup at the table over your "tomato sandwiches."

CHEF
Derrick VanDuzer

crispy tripe sandwich
with vegetable sotto aceto

YIELDS 4 SERVINGS

TRIPE

2 lbs. beef tripe, cleaned

1 onion, sliced

2 celery stalks

1 carrot

2 Tbsp. butter

2 Tbsp. olive oil

1 tsp. pepper flakes

1 cup white wine

1 qt. chicken stock

2 cups tomato sauce

1 sprig thyme

1 sprig rosemary

2 bay leaves

¼ cup red wine vinegar

Salt and pepper, to taste

3 eggs

2 Tbsp. water

1 Tbsp. harissa

2 cups panko
  breadcrumbs

VEGETABLES

1 qt. rice vinegar

2 cups sugar

1 tsp. fennel seed

1 tsp. chili flakes

1 red pepper, cut into strips

1 yellow pepper, cut into strips

1 fennel bulb, cut into strips

10 baby carrots, peeled

10 baby red onions, peeled

1 cup cauliflower florets

SPICY DRESSING

1 egg yolk

2 tsp. harissa paste

2 Tbsp. lemon juice

2 Tbsp. water

¾ cup olive oil

Salt and pepper, to taste

SANDWICH

1 qt. corn oil

1-2 loaves of focaccia or
  ciabatta bread

Roasted peppers, as needed

1 cup baby greens (dressed
  with olive oil and vinegar)

METHOD

Bring a large pot of water to a boil. Blanch the tripe by plunging it into the water and cooking 1 minute. Change the water and repeat 3 times. Place tripe on a plate and refrigerate until cool. Remove the tripe from the refrigerator and cut into 4 x 4 inch squares.

In a medium deep braising pot, sweat the onions, carrots, and celery in the olive oil and butter. After about 3 minutes, add the pepper flakes and the tripe. Deglaze with the white wine and reduce until wine is evaporated. Cover with the chicken stock and tomato sauce. Add the herbs, vinegar, salt, and pepper. Cover and braise 3 - 4 hours or until the tripe is tender. This can be stored up to 3 days. Crack the eggs into a small bowl. Add the water and harissa and beat together to make an egg wash. Dip the tripe squares into the egg wash and then into the panko bread crumbs. Reserve.

To make the spicy dressing, place the egg yolk in a small bowl with the liquids. Add the olive oil slowly, and combine till thick. Season with salt and pepper. Reserve.

To pickle the vegetables, bring the rice wine vinegar to a boil and add the sugar. Stir until it dissolves. Add the fennel seed and chili flakes. Pour the hot liquid over the vegetables and place in the refrigerator. This can be made up to 1 week in advance.

To make the sandwich, heat the oil in a medium deep sauce pot till 375°. Fry each piece of tripe until it is crispy and season with salt and pepper. Cut your bread into the desired width and slice in half. Brush some olive oil on the inside part of the sandwich and toast on a grill, in the oven, or in the toaster oven. Place the piece of tripe, still warm, on the bottom piece of the bread. Add roasted peppers and greens and finally the spicy dressing. Serve with the vegetables sotto aceto on the side.

CHEF / OWNER
Andrew Carmellini

media noche inside out

requires advanced preperation

YIELDS 2 SANDWICHES

PORK BELLY BRINE

5 cups water	1 cup coriander seeds
2 cups kosher salt	6 sticks cinnamon
1 tsp. sel rose	2 cloves
3 cloves garlic, crushed	1 dried bay leaf
Zest of 1 orange	3 sprigs thyme
Zest of 1 lemon	2 juniper berries
1 star anise	2 allspice
	5 lbs. fresh pork belly, with skin

METHOD

Add all ingredients, except the pork belly, to a pot and slowly bring to a boil. Remove from heat and cool completely. Lay the pork belly flat into a container and cover with the brine. Refrigerate for 24 hours. Rinse in cool water for 1 hour. Cry-o-vac and cook at 140° for 46 hours.

SOY SHERRY GASTRIQUE

1 cup sugar

1 cup sherry vinegar

1 cup soy sauce

2 star anise

2 tsp. coarsely ground black pepper

1 tsp. crushed red pepper flakes

ASSEMBLY

6 persimmon slices, grilled

2 country bread slices, toasted

4 scallions, blanched and grilled

METHOD

Add sugar to a heavy bottomed pot large enough to accommodate all of the ingredients and mix just enough water into the sugar until it attains a wet sand consistency. Caramelize the sugar over moderate heat to a deep golden color. Remove the caramel from the stove and slowly add the vinegar, followed by the soy sauce. Add the remaining ingredients and simmer gently until thick.

Cut the pork belly into 4 equal squares. Slowly render the pork belly in a heavy bottomed sauté pan skin side first. Transfer to a 300° oven to heat through. The skin should be very crisp when finished. Remove the crisp skin from the portions of pork belly and set aside. Cut the meat and fat into thick slices. Layer the grilled persimmons and pork belly around the toasted bread, and liberally drizzle with the gastrique. Cap off both ends with the crisp crackling. Garnish with the grilled scallions.

AUREOLE

EXECUTIVE CHEF

Tony Aiazzi

braised short ribs
on talegio baguette

SHORT RIBS

1 Tbsp. cayenne pepper

1 Tbsp. smoked paprika

1 Tbsp. crushed black pepper

1 Tbsp. chili powder

4 Tbsp. salt

10 lbs. beef short ribs

2 onions, roughly chopped

2 carrots, roughly chopped

1 stalk celery, roughly chopped

Vegetable oil, as needed

8 oz. tomato paste

2 cups red wine

1½ gallons beef stock

2 cloves of garlic

1 bay leaf

2 star anise

Fresh thyme, to taste

SANDWICH

1 cup Hellmann's mayo

1 Tbsp. chopped chives

1 baguette

1 bunch fresh watercress

Salt and pepper, to taste

White truffle oil, as needed

Boneless short ribs, reheated in jus

Talegio cheese, room temperature, to taste

METHOD

Mix together the cayenne, paprika, black pepper, chili powder, and salt. Rub the spice mix all over the ribs. Sear all sides of the ribs in heavy bottomed pot and set aside. Sauté the onions, celery, and carrots in vegetable oil over medium heat until the onions are translucent. Add the tomato paste. Stir and allow tomato paste to cook, approximately 15 minutes. Add the red wine and reduce by half. Add the beef stock, garlic, bay leaf, star anise, and short ribs and simmer over low heat for approximately 2 1/2 hours. Add the thyme and allow ribs to cool in stock. Remove short ribs from the pot and trim away the bones and cartilage (short rib scraps make great chilli!). Strain the jus and skim off fat.

Mix mayo with chopped chives and 1/2 cup of short rib jus. Spread mayo mix on toasted baguette. Season the watercress with salt, pepper, and white truffle oil. Lay out the boneless short ribs on baguette, topped with Talegio cheese. Toast in oven at 375° for 6 minutes. Top with watercress and other slice of baguette.

DAVID BURKE at bloomingdale's

EXECUTIVE CHEF
Chris Shea

lobster roll

INGREDIENTS

2 lbs. cooked lobster meat, chopped
    roughly into ½ and ¾ inch pieces
½ celery rib, finely chopped
¼ cup Hellmann's mayonnaise
Squeeze of lemon juice
Pinch of salt and freshly ground
    black pepper, to taste
2 tsp. unsalted butter
2 Pepperidge Farm top-loading
    hot dog buns
Chopped chives, for garnish

METHOD

In a large bowl, combine the lobster meat, celery, mayonnaise, lemon, salt and pepper and mix thoroughly. Cover the mixture and store it in the refrigerator until ready to serve. It will last for up to two days.

In a small sauté pan over low to medium heat, melt the butter. Place the hot dog buns on their sides in the butter. Flip the buns a couple of times so that both sides soak up an equal amount of butter and brown evenly. Remove the buns from the pan and place them on a large plate. Fill the toasted buns with the lobster salad. Sprinkle with chives and serve with a salad, slaw or shoestring fries.

Variation: For a shrimp roll, substitute 2 lbs. of shrimp, cooked, peeled and sliced in half lengthwise.

EXECUTIVE CHEF
Rebecca Charles

salad on flatbread

INGREDIENTS

1 carrot

1 stalk celery

2 stalks asparagus

Sugar snap peas

1 tomato

1 beet

Olive oil, as needed

Salt and pepper, to taste

2 slices flatbread

METHOD

Slice the carrots, celery and asparagus with a peeler. Cut the sugar snap peas in half (not lengthwise) and thinly cut up the tomato and beet. Mix all the vegetables with olive oil and season with salt and pepper. Take a slice of flat bread and put some of your vegetable mixture on top. Place the another slice of flatbread atop your vegetables.

sardine sandwich

YIELDS 2 SANDWICHES

INGREDIENTS

4 fresh sardines, filleted with head on

Salt and pepper, to taste

Extra virgin olive oil, as needed

1 preserved lemon, thinly sliced

1 large ripe tomato, thinly sliced

1 Tbsp. capers

¼ cup pine nuts

METHOD

Place sardine filets on oven proof baking dish and season with salt and pepper and drizzle with olive oil. Place under broiler and cook for 5 minutes.

Remove one filet onto serving dish and top with sliced lemon, tomato, capers, and pine nuts. Top off with the other filet and drizzle with olive oil, creating a sandwich.

GUSTO

ristorante e bar americano

EXECUTIVE CHEF
Amanda Freitag

oxtail salad

SERVES 1

INGREDIENTS

1 oxtail

Vegetable oil, as needed

4 whole carrots, peeled

2 whole onions, peeled

1 cup red wine

3 cups veal stock

6 cloves garlic

3 bay leaves

1 apple, diced into ⅛ inch pieces

1 cooked potato, peeled and
    diced into ⅛ inch pieces

1 Tbsp. heavy cream

1 Tbsp. chopped chives

1 splash of red wine vinegar

Salt & pepper, to taste

METHOD

Sear the oxtail in vegetable oil and then place into a 3 inch deep curved roasting pan. In a separate pan, clean and dice carrots and onions and roast until brown. Add red wine and reduce by half. Add veal stock, garlic, bay leaves and the oxtail. Roast in 350° oven for 2-3 hours, or until tender. In a bowl, mix diced apple, potato, heavy cream, chives and red wine vinegar. Add salt and pepper to taste and set aside. Remove oxtail from pot and let cool. Pull meat of oxtail apart and put in a separate bowl. Strain sauce and reduce by half. Spoon as desired into shredded oxtail to moisten.

ASSEMBLY

Take apple and potato mixture and arrange as desired on a plate with desired bread to form a sandwich. Arrange oxtail on top of potato/apple. Serve immediately.

Le Petit Chateau

CHEF / OWNER
Scott Cutaneo

SANDWICHES

one mean panini

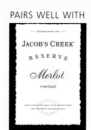
YIELDS 4 TO 8 SERVINGS

INGREDIENTS

1 loaf ciabatta

3 Tbsp. olive oil (for sandwich)

1 Tbsp. olive oil (for arugula)
    plus more for oiling grill

7 oz. (12 slices) prosciutto cotto

3 oz. (12 slices) Genoa salami

5 oz. (10 slices) fontina

3 ½ oz. (5 slices) mortadella

4 oz. (10 slices) spicy cappicola

7 oz. (8 slices) fresh mozzarella

1 (7 oz.) container chicken and duck pâté

3 ½ oz. shredded duck confit

1 ½ oz. (8 slices) speck

4 oz. (5 slices) Brie

2 ½ oz. (5 slices) prosciutto

2 oz. arugula

Salt and ground black pepper, to taste

METHOD

Slice the bread in 1/2 lengthwise. Drizzle the cut side of the bottom half with 3 Tbsp. olive oil. Layer the prosciutto cotto on the bottom half. Top with salami, fontina, mortadella, cappicola and mozzarella. Spoon the pâté on top. Press the confit into the pâté. Top with the speck, brie and prosciutto. Place the other half of the bread on top.

Prepare a grill or heat a large grill pan over medium-high heat. Once hot, oil it lightly. Put the sandwich on the grill for 5 minutes. Place a heavy cast iron pan on top to press. Cook for another 5 minutes. Remove from the grill.

Toss the arugula with 1 Tbsp. olive oil, salt and pepper. Remove the top half of the bread. Arrange the arugula on top of the prosciutto. Replace the bread. Slice into 4 large pieces or 8 small ones.

CHEF / OWNER
Emeril Lagasse

crispy rotisserie pork sandwich
with kimchee, takuan and scallion tofu sauce

a n n i s a

CHEF / OWNER   CREATED WITH

Anita Lo   Soa Davies

PORK BELLY
2 lbs. fresh pork belly, skin on

Salt and pepper, to taste

Vegetable oil, as needed

TOFU SAUCE
⅓ cup silken tofu

2 stalks scallion greens, blanched,
   shocked and dried

1 Tbsp. white soy

SANDWICH
4 Chinese steamed buns, halved

Kimchee leaves, as needed

16 slices takuan (Japanese pickled daikon)

1 stalk scallion (white part only), julienned

METHOD
Season the pork on both sides and tie with butcher string into a tight roll, skin side out. Brush the outside with a thin layer of oil and place on a rotisserie skewer. Roast slowly, turning constantly until soft, about 3 1/2-4 hours. Raise the heat to high (stop the rotation if necessary) to crisp the skin until it bubbles. Allow it to rest and then slice.

Make the tofu sauce by placing the tofu, blanched scallion greens and white soy in a blender and blend until smooth.
Season to taste with salt and pepper.

To form each sandwich, steam the bread until soft and place a heaping tablespoon of the tofu sauce on one side of the bun.
Top with the kimchee, daikon, scallion, and warm pork slices.
Serve immediately.

big pretzel panini

INGREDIENTS

Dijon mayonnaise (recipe follows)

1 piece pretzel bread

1 grilled chicken breast

1 large tomato slice

4 slices good quality provolone

4 slices crispy applewood smoked bacon

DIJON MAYONNAISE

1 cup mayo

1 cup Dijon Pomeroy mustard

Salt and pepper, to taste

1 Tbsp. mustard oil

METHOD

Mix together the Dijon mayonnaise ingredients. Slice bread in half. Brush both sides with mayonnaise.

Layer sandwich in the following order: chicken, tomato, provolone, bacon, then put in sandwich press till cheese melts. Do not let the bread burn.

SANDWICHES of the WORLD

EXECUTIVE CHEF

David Burke

PAIRS WELL WITH

ROYAL
ESMERALDA
AGED 20 YEARS
FINE DRY AMONTILLADO
SHERRY

SANDEMAN

roasted loin of pork on banana bread

requires advanced preperation

INGREDIENTS

2 lb. pork loin

Pork marinade (recipe follows)

Olive oil, as needed (for searing the pork loin)

Banana bread (recipe follows)

1 green plantain, julienned (for fries)

Vegetable oil, as needed (for frying the plantains)

1 red onion, sliced and grilled

Romaine lettuce leaves, as needed

Fruit chutney (recipe follows)

METHOD

In a mixing bowl combine all of the marinade ingredients, place the pork loin in the marinade and refrigerate overnight. When done marinating roast the pork loin in a fry pan with olive oil over high heat to sear on all sides. Place the pork loin in a pre-heated 350° oven and roast until the internal temperature of the pork reaches 160°. Remove from oven and let the meat rest before slicing.

THE FOUR SEASONS
RESTAURANT

EXECUTIVE CHEF
Christian Albin

CHEF DE CUISINE
Fred Mero

CHEF DE CUISINE
Peco Zantilaveevan

MARINADE FOR THE PORK LOIN

¼ oz. cilantro, roughly chopped

1¼ oz. chopped garlic

4 Tbsp. tomato ketchup

2 Tbsp. oyster sauce

3 Tbsp. ketjup manis (sweet soy sauce)

1 Tbsp. honey

2 cinnamon sticks

½ tsp. black pepper

6 oz. grenadine

Juice of half a lime

BANANA BREAD

4 ripe bananas, mashed

1 cup rice flour

1 cup potato starch

1¼ cup unsweetened coconut milk

1 Tbsp. sugar

1 tsp. salt

1 Tbsp. unsweetened shredded coconut

FRUIT CHUTNEY

2¼ cups Rose's lime juice

1¼ cups pineapple juice

6 Tbsp. rice vinegar

6 Tbsp. mirin

1½ cups sweet chili sauce

1 Tbsp. curry powder

1 Tbsp. turmeric

5 Tbsp. sugar

3 oz. brown sugar

1 oz. minced fresh ginger

1 tsp. minced fresh garlic

5 Tbsp. cornstarch

6 Tbsp. water

3 oz. black raisins

2 oz. small diced red onion

2¼ oz. diced red peppers

1 lb. small diced ripe pineapple

1 lb. small diced ripe mango

Chopped scallions and/or cilantro
to taste, (optional)

METHOD

Combine all the ingredients in a mixing bowl. Place mixture in a greased 9x12" baking pan covered with aluminum foil. Place in a steamer or bain-marie and cook for 20 minutes. The bread will be sticky but firm. Allow it to cool, remove from the pan and cut into slices for the sandwich.

METHOD

In a large sauce pot bring the lime juice, pineapple juice, rice vinegar, mirin and chili sauce to a simmer. Mix in the curry, turmeric, sugars, ginger and garlic and cook until reduced by half. In a bowl, whisk the cornstarch with the water making sure that there are no lumps. Add the cornstarch mixture to the pot (this will thicken the chutney). Add the raisins, onion, red peppers and pineapple. Cook until the pineapple is translucent but not mushy. Remove from heat and fold in the mango (the heat will cook the mangos). You can also add chopped cilantro and scallions to taste before serving.

For the plantain chips, julienne green plantains and fry in 350° vegetable oil until golden brown and crisp. Remove from the oil, place on paper towels and season with salt.

Assemble the sandwich with the grilled onion slices and romaine lettuce.

chicken shawarma
with hummus and pickled vegetables

SANDWICHES of the WORLD

SERVES 4

INGREDIENTS

Marinade:

½ cup yogurt

2 Tbsp. lemon juice

1 Tbsp. white wine vinegar

3 cloves garlic, minced

1 Tbsp. onion, finely minced

1 bay leaf

1 tsp. salt

3 tsp. shawarma spice*

¼ tsp. cayenne pepper

or make your own spice

2 tsp. curry powder

¼ tsp. cinnamon

¼ tsp. nutmeg

¼ tsp. cardamom

¼ tsp. cayenne pepper

MEAT

1 lb. chicken breast, thinly sliced

2 Tbsp. olive oil

GARNISH

4 pieces pita bread

1 cup hummus*

2 cups French fries

*Available at Middle Eastern markets

PICKLED VEGETABLES

Carrots	1 cup julienned carrots	Onions	1 cup thinly sliced onions
	1 Tbsp. white wine vinegar		1 Tbsp. lemon juice
	½ tsp. salt		½ tsp. salt
	1 Tbsp. chopped mint		½ tsp. cayenne pepper
Cabbage	1 cup shredded cabbage	Peppers	1 cup of julienned red bell peppers
	1 Tbsp. white wine vinegar		1 cup red wine vinegar
	½ tsp. salt		2 Tbsp. sugar
	1 tsp. curry powder		1 bay leaf
	¼ tsp. turmeric		1¼ tsp. black peppercorns

METHOD

Combine the ingredients for the marinade in a mixing bowl. Add sliced chicken, mix well, and marinate for at least 4 hours. Place carrots in a mixing bowl and add 1 Tbsp. white wine vinegar and 1/2 tsp. salt. Add 1 tsp. chopped mint. Leave to stand 2-3 hours. Place onions in a mixing bowl and add 1 Tbsp. lemon juice and 1/2 tsp. salt. Add 1/2 tsp. cayenne pepper. Leave to stand 2-3 hours. Place cabbage in a mixing bowl and add 1 Tbsp. white wine vinegar and 1/2 tsp. salt. Add 1 tsp. curry powder and 1/4 tsp. turmeric. Leave to stand 2-3 hours. Place peppers in a clean plastic container with a lid. Bring 1 cup red wine vinegar, 2 Tbsp. sugar, 1 bay leaf, and 1/4 tsp. whole peppercorns to a boil. Pour over peppers and cover. Leave to stand 2-3 hours.

Heat a large skillet over high flame. Add 2 Tbsp. olive oil and marinated chicken. Sauté until chicken is cooked through and slightly brown.

Split pita breads open. With a spoon, spread a layer of hummus on the inside of each pita. Next, fill each pita up with chicken meat and French fries. Top off with pickled vegetables.

BARBOUNIA

EXECUTIVE CHEF

Timothy Reardon

SANDEMAN
IMPORE
RUBY PORTO

tea sandwiches

BLACKBERRY SEMIFREDDO

8 oz. white chocolate

4 oz. butter

6 egg yolks

2 ½ oz. sugar

2 ½ oz. blackberry purée

1 oz. blackberry brandy

36 oz. heavy cream,
    whipped to soft peaks

METHOD

Place the chocolate and butter in a bowl, melt over a bain marie, and set aside. In another bowl, combine the egg yolks, sugar, blackberry purée and brandy, set over a bain marie and whisk until mixture is hot to the touch and slightly thickened. Then mix on a stand mixer using the whisk attachment on high speed. When the mixture has cooled slightly, add the chocolate and butter and whisk until cool. Fold in the whipped cream. Pour into a loaf pan lined with plastic wrap and freeze. Slice thinly to make the sandwiches.

ASSEMBLY

Trim the crusts from the pound cakes and cut into slices. Cut the slices into triangles. Using the cake triangles as "bread," spread the Blackberry Semifreddo between two triangles of the lemon pound cake and the Dark Chocolate Semifreddo between two triangles of the chocolate pound cake. Serve immediately with mixed berries for garnish.

PASTRY CHEF
Maggie Huff

DARK CHOCOLATE SEMIFREDDO

8 oz. 72% chocolate

4 oz. butter

6 egg yolks

2 ½ oz. sugar

3 ½ oz. Godiva liqueur

36 oz. heavy cream,
    whipped to soft peaks

Ground pistachios, as needed

METHOD

Place the chocolate and butter in a bowl, melt over a bain marie and set aside. In another bowl, combine the egg yolks, sugar, Godiva liqueur, set over a bain marie and whisk until the mixture is hot to the touch and slightly thickened. Then mix on a stand mixer using the whisk attachment on high speed. When the mixture has cooled slightly, add the chocolate and butter and whisk until cool. Fold in the whipped cream. Pour into a loaf pan lined with plastic wrap and freeze. Slice very thinly to make the sandwiches. Roll the edges in toasted ground pistachios.

CHOCOLATE POUND CAKE

2 ½ cups cake flour

½ cup cocoa powder

½ tsp. baking soda

½ tsp. salt

1 cup butter

3 cups sugar

6 eggs

1 cup melted dark chocolate

METHOD

Sift together dry ingredients and set aside. Mix butter and sugar in an electric mixer until light and fluffy. Mix in the eggs, one at a time. Stir in dry ingredients and then add the melted chocolate. Pour into prepared loaf pan and bake at 350° for 35-45 minutes. Cool slightly in pan, then finish cooling on a rack. Refrigerate or freeze cake until very firm so you can trim away the outside crust, and slice very thin for the sandwiches.

TANGY LEMON POUND CAKE

3 cups cake flour

½ tsp. baking soda

½ tsp. salt

1 cup goats milk butter

3 cups sugar

6 eggs

1 Tbsp. lemon zest

¼ cup lemon juice

1 cup labneh or Greek yogurt

METHOD

Sift together dry ingredients and set aside. Mix butter and sugar in an electric mixer until light and fluffy. Mix in the eggs, one at a time. Add the zest and lemon juice. Stir in the dry ingredients and then add the labneh. Pour into prepared loaf pan and bake at 350° for 35-45 minutes. Cool slightly in pan, then finish cooling on a rack. Refrigerate or freeze the cake until very firm so you can trim away the outside crust and slice very thin for the sandwiches.

gluten-free brick oven siciliano chicken

requires advanced preperation

YIELDS APPROX 6 SANDWICHES

GLUTEN-FREE BREAD (1 ½ LB LOAF)

1 Tbsp. gluten free dry yeast	¼ cup cornstarch
1 ¾ cups warm water	¼ cup millet flour
1 tsp. sugar	¼ cup garbanzo flour
Dry skimmed milk	¼ cup fava flour
¼ cup honey	¾ cup sorghum flour
1 whole egg	½ cup brown rice flour
2 egg whites	½ cup white rice flour
¼ cup canola oil	1 Tbsp. xanthan gum
½ cup tapioca flour	1 ½ tsp. salt

METHOD

Mix dry yeast with warm water and 1 tsp. of sugar. Wait until the yeast begins to foam. Add the wet ingredients to the bowl. Add the dry ingredients to the bowl. Using a dough hook, mix the product until you achieve a nice smooth consistency. Place the mixture into a loaf pan and allow to rise for 30 minutes or until the loaf doubles in size. Bake 15-25 minutes at 350°. The top should have a nice brown crust.

EXECUTIVE CHEF
Ron Malina

CHIPOTLE PEPPER AIOLI

¼ cup sliced onions	2-3 dried chipotle chilies, stems
Vegetable oil, as needed	removed, sliced lengthwise
3 cloves garlic, sliced	2 Tbsp. cider vinegar
¼ cup fresh chopped tomatoes	Pinch of sugar
2-3 cups water	3-4 cups mayonnaise
	Salt and pepper, to taste

Sauté onions in vegetable oil until light brown in color. Add garlic and tomatoes and sauté 1-2 minutes longer. Add 2-3 cups of water, chipotles, vinegar and sugar. Cook covered under low heat until the chipotles are soft and the mixture is reduced and thickened. Allow to cool. Add the mixture to 4 cups of your favorite mayonnaise and blend with a hand mixer. Add salt and pepper, to taste.

SPICY BUFFALO SAUCE

½ cup red hot sauce	1 Tbsp. honey
(cayenne pepper sauce)	1-2 cloves garlic, crushed
⅓ cup butter	Salt and pepper, to taste

Combine all of the ingredients in a sauce pan and stir on low heat until the butter melts.

GRILLED CHICKEN

	1 tsp. salt
¼ cup olive oil	½ tsp. black pepper
2 garlic cloves, minced	1 tsp. sweet paprika
2 tsp. onion powder	2 ½ lbs. boneless chicken breast

Combine ingredients, spread over chicken and refridgerate overnight. Grill the following day.

salmon tartar
with roasted garlic oil on grilled sushi rice

SERVES 2

INGREDIENTS

1 cup sushi rice

2 Tbsp. rice vinegar

1 Tbsp. sugar

½ Tbsp. salt, plus extra as needed

¼ cup vegetable oil

4 cloves garlic

8 oz. wild salmon, minced

1 Tbsp. minced roasted shishito pepper

½ Tbsp. grated yuzu rind

3 Tbsp. finely chopped chives

METHOD

Cook the rice according to manufacturer's directions. While the rice is cooking, prepare the vinegar. In a small, non-reactive saucepot over medium heat, heat the rice vinegar until it is hot enough to dissolve the sugar and salt. Remove the vinegar mixture from the heat and let cool. Once the rice is done fold it into the vinegar mixture using a rubber spatula. Cover the rice with plastic wrap and set aside.

In a saucepot over medium heat add the vegetable oil and garlic cloves. Cook until the garlic is soft and golden and the oil is nutty and fragrant. Remove the oil from the heat and allow it to cool.

In a non-reactive mixing bowl combine the salmon, pepper, yuzu, chives and 2 Tbsp. of the garlic oil. Season the tartar well with salt.

Using a ring mold 4 inches in diameter, make four discs of sushi rice approximately 1/2 inch thick. Using a butane torch, or the broiler in your oven, char the outside of each disc on all sides. Spread half of the salmon mixture on one disc, as if spreading peanut butter on a slice of bread. Using another disc, as a slice of "bread", complete the first sandwich. Repeat to make the second sandwich. Cut each sandwich in half and drizzle with the remaining garlic oil. Serve with pieces of garlic on the side.

NOTE FROM THE CHEF

This recipe makes a nice lunch for two served with a salad, or as an appetizer for four.

EXECUTIVE CHEF
Jake Klein

banh mi

HOMEMADE PÂTÉ

2 tsp. vegetable oil

2 tsp. finely chopped onion

8 oz. ground pork

8 oz. finely chopped pork or veal liver

1 Tbsp. roast pork seasoning mix
(available in Asian markets)

1 tsp. 5-spice powder

2 tsp. sugar

2 tsp. soy sauce

2 tsp. Chinese cooking wine

Pinch of salt

Pinch of garlic powder

Pinch of ground black pepper

METHOD

Heat the oil in a small, nonstick skillet over medium heat. Add the onion and cook, stirring, until soft. Add the remaining ingredients, and cook, stirring, until just cooked through, about 2 to 3 minutes. Remove from the heat and set aside covered with foil, to keep warm.

SLAW

½ cup water

¼ cup sugar

¼ cup distilled white vinegar

½ cup julienned carrots

½ cup julienned daikon radish

Kosher salt, to taste

SANDWICHES

10 (10-inch) baguettes

Mayonnaise, as needed

20 thin slices Vietnamese-style pork
roll (cha lua), or bologna

20 slices Vietnamese-style salami,
ham or turkey

10 tsp. soy sauce

1 cup fresh cilantro sprigs

1 medium English cucumber,
cut lengthwise into 10 slices

Freshly ground black pepper, to taste

Asian-style chili sauce, to taste (optional)

METHOD

In a small saucepan, combine water, sugar, and vinegar and bring to a boil. Transfer the vinegar mixture to a bowl and cool. Add the carrots and daikon, mix well and season with salt. Set aside to marinate for 30 minutes or store in the refrigerator up to overnight.

METHOD

Preheat the oven to 400°. Slice the baguettes lengthwise and slather the insides with mayonnaise. Arrange the baguettes on a baking sheet and bake until crusty, about 5 minutes. Remove the baguettes from the oven and immediately fill each with some of the seasoned pâté. In each sandwich, arrange 2 slices each of the pork roll and salami, 1 tsp. soy sauce, 1/2 Tbsp. cilantro, 1 slice cucumber, ground pepper, and chili sauce, if using. Serve immediately with slaw on the side.

EXECUTIVE CHEF

Michael Bao Huynh

white sturgeon burger
on brioche caviar crème

STURGEON BURGER

1 Tbsp. olive oil

4-5 oz. boneless sturgeon filets

Salt and pepper, to taste

4 Petrossian brioche buns

1 tsp. butter

½ cup crème fraiche

1 Tbsp. transmontanus caviar

1 vine ripe tomato, sliced

Baby greens, as needed

Cornichons, as needed (for garnish)

ZUCCHINI FRIES

2 medium zucchini

Flour, as needed (for dredging)

3 eggs, whites only

2 cups panko bread crumbs

16 oz. canola oil (for frying)

Salt and pepper, to taste

METHOD

Preheat frying oil to 375˚.

Place sauté pan on high heat and add olive oil. Season the sturgeon with salt and pepper and add to smoking pan. Reduce heat to medium and cook for two minutes and then flip until sturgeon is cooked through. In the meantime, brush rolls with melted butter and grill. If you do not have a grill, toast the bread until golden brown and brush with melted butter. Set aside. In a stainless steel bowl, mix the crème fraiche and the caviar together. Be careful not to over mix. It is important that the crème fraiche remains white and the caviar is identifiable.

METHOD

Slice the zucchini on a diagonal about 1 centimeter thick. Dredge in flour, then egg white and then fine panko bread crumbs. Fry in canola oil until golden brown. Season with salt and pepper.

ASSEMBLY

Spread caviar mixture onto toasted rolls. Create your sandwich by stacking the fish, tomato and greens. Serve with remaining caviar crème, cornichons and fries.

EXECUTIVE CHEF
Michael Lipp

the battman blt

YIELDS 4 SERVINGS

BRAISED PORK BELLY

2 lbs. pork belly

2 cups BHM Townsend's salt cure

1 onion, small dice

2 ribs celery, small dice

1 carrot, small dice

1 Tbsp. tomato paste

1 qt. white wine

4 qts. veal stock

6 thyme sprigs

4 rosemary sprigs

1 bay leaf

Salt and pepper, to taste

METHOD

Remove skin from pork belly and score top diagonally. Spread cure around belly, cover, and let sit for 12 hours. Rinse and pat dry. Slowly render scored side in stainless steel pan. Develop deep brown sear on all sides. Remove excess fat from pan.

Sauté vegetables till soft and lightly caramelized. Add tomato paste and continue to caramelize. Deglaze with wine. Reduce by 3/4. Add veal stock.

Arrange belly in roasting pan. Spread fresh herbs around pan. Add salt and pepper. Add liquid till pork is almost covered. Bring to a boil. Cover with foil. Braise in oven at 300° till fork tender. Cool and store in cooking liquid.

SANDWICH

8 pieces of braised pork belly, cut into ¼ inch slices

4 Tbsp. basil-tarragon mayo

8 pieces of white bread, toasted

8 leaves red leaf lettuce

1 yellow or red tomato, cut into ½ inch slices

Salt and pepper, to taste

BASIL & TARRAGON MAYO

½ bunch basil, chopped

½ bunch tarragon, chopped

1 cup good quality mayonnaise

METHOD

Heat a stainless steel pan to medium-low. Add pork belly and lightly sear for 2 minutes per side. Remove from heat and place on a paper towel to drain. Spread mayo on one side of each piece of toasted white bread. Place 2 pieces of pork belly on top of half of the slices. Add lettuce. Season tomato slices with salt and pepper to taste. Place 2 slices of tomato on each sandwich. Top with remaining slices.

METHOD

Combine all ingredients.

EXECUTIVE CHEF
Kenny Callaghan

PAIRS WELL WITH

─── ESTABLISHED 1847 ───

JACOB'S CREEK®

CHARDONNAY

VINTAGE

NAMED AFTER JACOB'S CREEK, SITE OF JOHANN GRAMP'S
FIRST VINEYARD IN THE BAROSSA VALLEY

jerk chicken sandwich

SANDWICHES of the WORLD

INGREDIENTS

1 roll

8 oz chicken breast

1 tsp. jerk marinade (store bought)

1 Tbsp. jerk sauce or steak sauce (store bought)

1 tsp. Dijon mustard

1 tsp. mayonnaise

¼ tsp. grated ginger

2 slices fresh pineapple

1 Tbsp. guava preserves (or your preference)

2 slices fresh avocado

1 romaine lettuce leaf

METHOD

Gently pound breast. Season with jerk marinade. Let it stand in refrigerator for approximately 2 hours. Combine steak or jerk sauce, Dijon mustard, mayonnaise and ginger and mix well. Grill chicken for approximately 5 minutes on each side. Grill pineapple slices for 1 minute on each side. Spread guava preserves on one side of roll and then spread the sauce mixture on the other side. Pile on chicken, pineapple, avocado and romaine lettuce.

NEGRIL VILLAGE

CHEF / OWNER
Marva Layne

grilled salted salmon
on grilled rice ball

YIELDS 1 SERVING

INGREDIENTS

1 tsp. salt

4 oz. salmon

1 cup Japanese rice, steamed

1 Tbsp. ao-nori flakes

1 tsp. sesame seeds, toasted

1 Tbsp. dry bonito flakes, finely copped

1 tsp. soy sauce

1 Shiso ohba

1 oz. watercress

1 snow crab leg meat

1 pinch Kaiware, radish sprouts

2 red radish slices

METHOD

Salt salmon 1 hour before cooking and then grill it. Mix the steamed rice with ao nori, sesame seeds, and bonito flakes. Make rice in a rounded triangular shape, the traditional Japanese rice ball shape. Grill rice ball with soy sauce until brown. Cut rice ball in 2 pieces lengthwise, to form a top and bottom (this is going be the "bread" of the sandwich). On one side of rice ball put shiso. Set salmon on top and cover with other piece of rice ball. Garnish with watercress, crabmeat, kaiware, and red radish.

MATSURI

EXECUTIVE CHEF
Tadashi Ono

pan bagnat

SERVES 4

INGREDIENTS

1 baguette (approximately 20-24 inches long)
    or 4 wide, round French rolls

1 garlic clove, peeled and halved

4 oz. homemade tapenade or prepared olive paste

1 large ripe tomato, sliced

1 red onion, sliced into rings

1 small head fennel, shaved and tossed with a little
    extra virgin olive oil and salt

2 hard cooked eggs, sliced

20 anchovy filets or 12 oz. good quality canned tuna

Red wine vinegar, as needed

Black pepper, to taste

Extra virgin olive oil, as needed

16 large basil leaves

METHOD

Split the bread in half and remove some of the white inside if it is doughy. Rub the bread with the clove of garlic. Spread the tapenade on evenly and then layer the tomatoes, onion rings, shaved fennel and hard cooked eggs, in that order. Add the anchovy filets or tuna, and season with a little red wine vinegar, black pepper and a liberal drizzle of olive oil over the top. Finish with the basil leaves. Place the top piece of bread on, wrap in plastic and place a plate on top. Put some weight on top of the plate to gently press the sandwich and refrigerate for up to one hour.

EXECUTIVE CHEF
Andy D'Amico

samba grilled sandwich

SERVES 4

INGREDIENTS

4 5-oz. tenderloin filets

2 tsp. sea salt

1 tsp. cracked black pepper

Cheese bread (recipe follows)

1 tomato

6 oz. goat cheese

Watercress, to garnish

METHOD

Seasoned the filets with the salt and black pepper. Grill the filets for 2 minutes on each side for medium rare.

CHEESE BREAD

1 cup water

1 cup milk

½ cup oil

1 tsp. salt

16 oz. tapioca starch

3 eggs

7 oz. grated Parmesan cheese

METHOD

Bring the water, milk, oil, and salt to a boil. Remove from heat and add tapioca starch. Mix well and let it cool down. Add the eggs and knead well. Add the grated cheese and keep kneading until the dough is smooth. Divide the entire mixture into balls of 2 Tbsp. each. Bake in 350° oven for about 30 minutes or until golden brown.

ASSEMBLY

Cut the cheese bread in half and assemble the filets, 1 slice of tomato, and 1 slice of goat cheese. Garnish with watercress and serve.

EXECUTIVE CHEF

Samire Soares

SANDWICHES of the WORLD

lamb sooley wraps

SANDWICHES of the WORLD

YIELDS 2 WRAPS

INGREDIENTS

½ lb. lamb (lean meat)

1 tsp. salt

2 tsp. ginger garlic paste

2 Tbsp. oil

1 tsp. garam marsala

¼ papaya

1 tsp. tomato shade (red food coloring)

Parantha (recipe follows)

METHOD

Cut the lamb into thin slices, season with salt, then add remaining ingredients. Let sit for 1 hour. Then put the lamb on skewers and cook it on a grill until done. Serve with tomato and mint chutney.

PARANTHA

Olive oil, as needed

2 cups wheat flour, plus extra as needed

6 oz. water

½ tsp. salt

METHOD

In the meantime, mix the ingredients for the parantha in a shallow bowl. Knead for about 3 minutes. Make 2 or more oblong pieces of dough like the size of an egg roll. Let rest for about 10 minutes.

Using a rolling pin and wheat flour as needed for dusting the board, roll the pieces of dough into round, not too thick discs. They should be about 10-12 inches in diameter. Heat the griddle for about 5 minutes and put 1/2 tsp. olive oil on the griddle so bread does not stick. Put bread on griddle and keep applying 1/2 tsp. of olive oil to keep it from sticking. Grill on slow fire until golden on both sides. Keep changing sides so it will not burn or get too crisp. It should not be hard, but pliable to use as a wrap.

tamarinD

EXECUTIVE CHEF   PASTRY CHEF

KB Singh   Claudio Quito

RIOJA

Campo Viejo
GRAN RESERVA
2000

PRODUCT OF SPAIN
RED WINE

grilled short rib sandwich

requires advanced preperation

INGREDIENTS

Horseradish mayonnaise (recipe follows)

1 sesame seeded baguette, sliced lengthwise, buttered and toasted

3 to 4 ¼-inch thick slices smoked mozzarella

Grilled short rib (amount to your liking, recipe follows)

3 to 4 slices red 0nion, grilled

3 to 4 halves roasted plum tomatoes (recipe follows)

10 to 12 leaves baby arugula, seasoned with olive oil, salt and pepper

HORSERADISH MAYONNAISE

1 cup real mayonnaise

1 oz. prepared horseradish

METHOD

Combine and reserve.

TOMATOES

4 plum tomatoes

Salt and pepper, to taste

Extra virgin olive oil, as needed

1 clove garlic, chopped

2 sprigs thyme, leaves picked

METHOD

Cut tomatoes in half. Season
with salt and pepper, drizzle
with olive oil, sprinkle garlic
and thyme and bake at 350°
for 15 minutes.

Ouest

CHEF / OWNER
Tom Valenti

SOUS CHEF
Scott Varricchio

BRAISED SHORT RIBS

1 (3-rib) piece of short rib

Coarse salt and freshly ground
black pepper, to taste

Garlic powder, as needed

1½ Tbsp., plus ¼ cup olive oil

1 rib celery, roughly chopped

½ carrot, roughly chopped

½ large Spanish onion,
roughly chopped

¼ cup tomato paste

1 sprig thyme

1 bay leaf

1 tsp. black peppercorns

1 anchovy filet

½ head garlic

1 cup red wine

½ cup dry white wine

¼ cup white vinegar

½ tsp sugar

1 cup veal stock or demi-glaze

1 cup chicken stock or water

METHOD

The day before cooking, score the fat covering the bones and season with salt, pepper, and the garlic powder. Cover with plastic wrap and refrigerator overnight. Preheat the oven to 325°. Warm the 1.5 Tbsp. oil in a roasting pan over medium high heat. Add the celery, carrot and onion and cook until very soft, about 5 minutes. Add the tomato paste and cook for 1-2 minutes. Add the thyme, bay leaf, peppercorns, anchovies and garlic, and cook another 2-3 minutes. Add the red and white wine, vinegar and sugar, raise the heat to high and bring to a boil. Lower the heat to medium and add the veal and chicken stocks. Leave over medium heat while you brown the ribs. Pour the remaining oil into a sauté pan and place over medium high heat. Add the ribs to the pan and brown on both sides, about 2 minute per side. Transfer the ribs to the roasting pan, bone side up, and pour the braising liquid over the top. Cover the pan with aluminum foil and cook in the preheated oven for 1 hour. Remove the foil and cook for 3 more hours, or until the bones are easy to remove and the meat is very soft. Turn the ribs over during the last 15 minutes to brown them a bit. Remove the ribs from the braising liquid and strain. Skim off all the fat you can from the liquid. Let ribs cool overnight in the refrigerator, then wrap in plastic for storage. Before serving, cut all sinew off of the ribs.

ASSEMBLY

Working from the bottom up, spread the horseradish mayo on both sides of the toasted bun. Lay sliced mozzarella across the bottom, then the grilled short rib, next the grilled red onion, then the roasted tomatoes and finally the arugula. Put the top half of the bun on and feel free to garnish with olives or dill pickles.

squid submarine sandwich

SANDWICHES of the WORLD

EXECUTIVE CHEF
Brad Steelman

INK BREAD

1 ½ oz. fresh brewer's yeast

½ cup milk

2 cups warm water

2 oz. melted butter

1 tsp. sugar

2 Tbsp. squid ink

2 lbs. all-purpose flour

1 tsp. salt

Eggs, as needed, beaten (for egg wash)

Sesame seeds, as needed (for sprinkling)

MEATBALLS

2 Tbsp. extra virgin olive oil

2 garlic cloves, minced

1 shallot, finely diced

Salt and fresh ground black pepper, to taste

2 lbs. cleaned fresh squid (tubes and tentacles)

1 Tbsp. chopped marjoram

1 Tbsp. chopped Italian parsley

¼ cup fresh breadcrumbs

Prepared tomato sauce, as needed

Flour, as needed

Olive oil, as needed

½ tsp. red chile flakes

METHOD

In the bowl of a mixer fitted with a dough hook, place all the ingredients except the flour and salt. Place mixer on low speed and allow the yeast to dissolve and the ingredients to incorporate. Add the flour and salt and mix into a ball. Cover the bowl with a dry towel and place in a warm area of the kitchen, allowing the dough to rise until nearly double in size. Punch down the dough and transfer to a floured work surface. Cut dough in to 3 oz. pieces and shape into oblong rolls. Place onto a lightly oiled baking sheet pan. Allow the dough to rise again, uncovered, until nearly doubled in size. Gently brush rolls with egg wash and sprinkle with sesame seeds. Bake the rolls in a pre heated 350° oven for approximately 10 minutes.

In a sauté pan over medium heat, add the extra virgin olive oil and garlic and cook until lightly golden. Add the shallots and season with salt and pepper. When the shallots are tender, remove the pan from the heat and allow to cool. Cut half the squid tubes into rings and reserve. Place all the remaining squid in a food processor fitted with the blade. With the machine on, drizzle in the shallot mixture, add herbs and breadcrumbs and season with salt and pepper. Shape into small meatballs and hold in the refrigerator.

Prepare your favorite tomato sauce recipe. Lightly dust the meatballs in flour and sauté in olive oil until golden. Simmer the meatballs in the sauce for 10 minutes and hold in warm sauce.

Season the reserved squid rings with salt, pepper, and chili flakes. In a sauté pan over high heat place a splash of olive oil and quickly sauté the rings taking care to not over cook. Split the top of an ink roll and fill with the simmered meatballs and sauce. Top with sautéed squid rings.

PAIRS WELL WITH

BRANCOTT
NEW ZEALAND

UNOAKED   *Gisborne*
CHARDONNAY

WINE OF NEW ZEALAND

country pâté sandwiches
with cucumber, tomatoes and anchovies

SERVES 4

INGREDIENTS

4 individual pieces of panini bread

3 tsp. olive oil

1 lb. of country pâté (duck, pork, etc.)
    or liverwurst

16 white anchovies

16 cherry tomatoes, cut into slices

1 seedless cucumber or Japanese cucumber,
    cut into ribbons

Salt and pepper, to taste

METHOD

Preheat a grill or grill pan. Slice panini in half lengthwise and brush with olive oil. Press the halves into grill and toast until crisp. Remove and allow to cool. Slice the pâté and lay it on the first half of the bread, top it with the anchovies lengthwise in the center. Add the tomato slices and cucumber ribbons (reserving a few of each for garnish) all around and let them drape slightly over the sides. Layer with the second piece of bread. Press and finish by topping with a line of cucumber ribbons and tomato down the length of the sandwich.

THE **MODERN**

EXECUTIVE CHEF
Gabriel Kreuther

lemongrass cured lamb sandwich

with snow pea ginger soup

YIELDS ABOUT 2 QUARTS OF SOUP

SNOW PEA GINGER SOUP

3 Tbsp. sesame oil

2 cups onion, medium dice

2 Tbsp. garlic, finely chopped

¼ cup fresh ginger, grated

4 Tbsp. lemongrass, chopped

3 lbs. fresh snow peas (place aside
   a few peas for garnish)

3 cups chicken or vegetable stock

2 12-oz. cans coconut milk

1 large potato, medium dice

4 oz. (2 handfuls) spinach

Salt and pepper, to taste

Sugar, to taste

3 Tbsp. cilantro, chopped

Snow pea shoots, for garnish

METHOD

Heat a medium stock pot. When hot, add the sesame oil and sauté the onions, garlic, ginger and lemongrass. Cook for approximately 3-5 minutes. Add the peas, chicken or vegetable stock, coconut milk and potato. (The potato is used to give the soup more body.) Allow the soup to simmer for 25 minutes. You may purée the soup in a food processor or blender. (A chef secret is to add spinach at this point; it gives the soup a vibrant green color.) Finally, add the salt, pepper, sugar and cilantro. For my garnish, I use julienne snow peas and snow pea shoots.

EXECUTIVE CHEF

Kenneth W. Collins

YIELDS 2 SANDWICHES

LEMONGRASS CURED LAMB

1 14-oz. lamb loin, cleaned

3 Tbsp. lemongrass, finely diced

2 Tbsp. shallots, finely diced

2 tsp. garlic, finely diced

2 Tbsp. cilantro, chopped

2 tsp. thyme, finely chopped

2 Tbsp. extra virgin olive oil

2 tsp. kosher salt

½ tsp. fresh ground pepper

4 portions focaccia bread (or any
   Tuscan, artesian bread preferred)

4 oz. arugula or mizuna lettuce

Olive oil, as needed

Salt and pepper, to taste

Sugar, to taste

1 tomato, sliced

1 mango, sliced

SWEET POTATO RIBBONS

(MAKES ENOUGH FOR 2)

1 jumbo sweet potato

1 quart canola oil

Salt, to taste

METHOD

Place the lamb on a sheet pan with parchment paper. Create a rub by incorporating the lemongrass, shallots, garlic, cilantro, thyme, olive oil, salt and ground pepper in a bowl and mix well. To marinate the lamb, spread the rub over the entire piece of meat and let it rest in the refrigerator for 1 hour. Grill or pan sear the lamb to the desired doneness. (Medium rare, takes about 3-4 minutes on each side.) Let rest for 2 minutes. (This prevents the meat from losing its juices.) Cut the lamb into thin slices.

Toss the lettuce with a touch of olive oil, salt, pepper and sugar.

Grill or heat the bread. You may want to build a single layer or a double decker. On the bottom half of the bread, place the arugula. Layer the tomatoes, mango and lamb. Use spear picks or chop sticks to hold the sandwich together and serve.

Using a potato peeler, peel the sweet potato in strips that resemble ribbons. Fry them in 350° oil, constantly moving them around until crisp. Remove from oil and place on a paper towels to absorb any excess oil. Season to taste with kosher salt.

BRANCOTT
MARLBOROUGH
SAUVIGNON BLANC
BRANCOTT

tartine de thon à la niçoise
tuna niçoise tartine

INGREDIENTS

1 ½ pounds good quality canned tuna, packed in olive oil

1 Tbsp. plus 1 tsp. minced shallots

1 Tbsp. plus 1 tsp. minced cornichons

1 Tbsp. plus 1 tsp. minced drained non pareil capers (preferably Spanish)

1 Tbsp. minced chives

2 tsp. minced Italian parsley

2 tsp. minced tarragon

2 tsp. minced chervil

1 Tbsp. fresh lemon juice

¾ cup mayonnaise

Kosher salt and freshly ground black pepper, to taste

1 pain de campagne (about 2 1x1 inch)

Extra virgin olive oil, as needed

Kosher salt, to taste

¼ cup aioli

12 to 16 small young Bibb lettuce leaves

Freshly ground black pepper, to taste

4 hard cooked large eggs

12 large radish slices

16 niçoise olives, pitted and halved

¼ cup minced chives

12 cornichons

4 small bunches mâche or watercress, or pommes frites (optional)

METHOD

Just as it's important to use perfectly cooked lamb or pork when making tartines featuring those ingredients, a good-quality canned tuna will make the difference between a good tuna salad and an excellent one. The salt content can vary from brand to brand so taste as you season.

Put the tuna in a strainer set over a bowl to allow excess oil to drain off but do not squeeze dry. Transfer the drained tuna to a large bowl and break it apart with a fork. Add the shallots, cornichons, capers, chives, parsley, tarragon, and chervil and toss together. Gently stir in the lemon juice and mayonnaise. Do not let the mixture become a paste. Season to taste with salt and pepper.

Preheat the broiler. Lay the pain de campagne on its side and cut it on a severe bias to get 4 slices approximately 10 inches long and 1/2 inch thick. Drizzle both sides of each slice lightly with olive oil and sprinkle with salt. Place under the broiler until golden brown on the first side, then turn to brown the second side.

Spread one side of each toast with 1 Tbsp. of aioli. Arrange the Bibb lettuce over the aioli and sprinkle with a pinch of salt and pepper. Mound the tuna salad down the length of each pain de campagne slice. Cut 4 slices from each egg and arrange the slices over the tunas. Season the egg with a pinch of salt. Arrange 3 radish slices over the egg slices on each pain de campagne. Press 3 olive halves into the tuna mixture on either side of each pain de campagne. Sprinkle 1 Tbsp. of chives over the top of each sandwich. Grind black pepper over the top of the sandwiched and drizzle with some olive oil.

Serve the tartines with cornichons, garnished with a small bunch of mâche or watercress, or if desired, .pommes frites.

BOUCHON

CHEF / PROPRIETOR
Thomas Keller

CHEF DE CUISINE
James Vellano

PAIRS WELL WITH

BRANCOTT
NEW ZEALAND

Marlborough
RIESLING

WINE OF NEW ZEALAND

choucroute sandwich

SERVES 4

INGREDIENTS

3 Tbsp. duck fat or butter

1 Spanish onion, thinly sliced

½ carrot

2 cloves of garlic

1 glass of Riesling

3 cups chicken stock

1 sachet d'epices (juniper berries, cloves,
     peppercorns, coriander seed)

1 bouquet garni (thyme, bay leaf, parsley)

½ lb. smoked bacon*

1 lb. good quality sauerkraut*

1 fresh pork tenderloin

2 bratwurst*

2 wieners*

2 weisswurst or knackwurst*

4 fresh baguettes

Dijon mustard, to taste

6 French breakfast radishes, sliced

8 cornichons, chopped

1 red onion, thinly sliced into rings

1 head frisée lettuce, washed and chopped

** These items can be obtained from most
   reputable German butchers.*

METHOD

In a large pot, heat the duck fat or butter. Add the sliced onion, carrot, and garlic cloves. Sweat briefly. Add the Riesling, chicken stock, sachet d'epices, bouquet garni, and smoked bacon. Bring to a simmer. Add the sauerkraut and mix well. Simmer for 30 minutes.

Roast the pork tenderloin until just cooked through. In the same pan, sauté the bratwurst until cooked through. Add the remaining sausages to the choucroute and simmer 10 more minutes. Remove from the heat. Remove the bacon, sausages, carrot, garlic, sachet and bouquet garni. Slice the bacon into 8 pieces, and each sausage into 4 pieces. Slice the tenderloin into 8 pieces.

ASSEMBLY

Split the baguette lengthwise, and brush both sides with mustard. Arrange a bed of the cooked choucroute on the bread, and top it with the 2 slices of each kind of sausage, 2 pieces of bacon, and 2 slices of the roasted tenderloin. Sprinkle with the radish slices, chopped cornichons, red onion, and frisée.

bistro moderne

EXECUTIVE CHEF
Olivier Muller

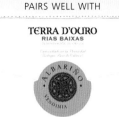

calf's liver pâté

YIELDS FOUR 5 OZ. SERVINGS

INGREDIENTS

1 calf's liver, peeled, chopped

3 oz. Swedish anchovies

2 oz. Swedish anchovy liquid

8 red onions, diced and caramelized

5 lbs. ground pork

1.1 lbs. flour

10 eggs

½ lb. diced fatback

13 ¼ oz. Swedish syrup

1 cup fresh marjoram, chopped

1 cup dried marjoram

21 oz. Sel rose (pink salt)

3 Tbsp. black pepper

2 ½ qts. heavy cream

Swedish-style pumpernickel bread,
   as needed

METHOD

In a robotcoup, purée the calf's liver, anchovies, anchovy liquid, and caramelized red onions. In a cold Hobart mixing bowl, with the paddle attachment, combine all of the ingredients except the cream and bread, and incorporate well. Slowly add the cream. Line pâté molds in plastic wrap, then bread and pour in mixture. Bake on combination (1/2 steam, 1/2 dry) heat at 220° until internal temperature is 145°. Press down with a weight and cool.

SANDWICHES of the WORLD

EXECUTIVE CHEF

Johan Svensson

soft shell club sandwich

eighty one

CHEF / OWNER
Ed Brown

YIELDS 4 SANDWICHES

INGREDIENTS

8 thick slices of quality bacon

8 medium soft shell crabs, dispatched and cleaned

½ cup all-purpose flour, for dredging

2 Tbsp. sweet butter

Salt, to taste

½ cup mayonnaise

½ cup pesto (recipe follows)

8 slices country loaf bread, lightly toasted

1 bunch arugula, washed and dried

1 small red onion, peeled, sliced into 4 inch thick slices

1 large red beefsteak tomato, cut into 4 inch thick slices

4 scallions, washed, quartered lengthwise

PESTO

10 clean basil leaves

½ bunch clean arugula leaves

1 ½ Tbsp. pine nuts

2 ½ tsp. grated Parmesan cheese

1 clove fresh garlic, peeled

¼ cup extra virgin olive oil

METHOD

To make the pesto, place all of the pesto ingredients in the bowl of a food processor. Process till smooth. Refrigerate.

In a large sauté pan at medium heat, cook bacon till crisp. Remove and keep warm. Discard half the fat, return pan to medium heat.

Dredge crabs lightly in flour, then sauté shell side down for 2 minutes. Flip the crabs, add the butter, and cook 2-1/2 minutes longer. Remove to paper towels and keep warm. Season with salt.

In a medium non-reactive bowl combine mayonnaise and pesto. Coat all slices of country bread liberally with the mayo mixture. Build the sandwich with the crabs, bacon, and remaining ingredients. Cut in half.

lamb burger on brioche

YIELDS 1 BURGER

INGREDIENTS

8 oz. ground lamb

1 shallot, diced

1 scallion, chopped, green & white part

3 cloves garlic confit

1 tsp. chopped parsley

1 tsp. chopped oregano

1 tsp. chopped dill

¼ tsp. crushed coriander

Salt and pepper, to taste

Caul fat for wrapping

Olive oil, as needed

Brioche bun

GARNISH

4 arugula leaves

1 slice sweet onion, grilled

4 thassos olives, pitted and diced

4 sun-dried tomatoes

2 Tbsp. crumbled feta cheese

Picked fresh dill and mint, to taste

1 tsp. lemon juice

1 tsp. extra virgin olive oil

Salt and pepper, to taste

METHOD

Preheat grill to medium-high heat. Combine the lamb, shallot, scallion, garlic, parsley, oregano, dill, coriander, salt, and pepper in a large mixing bowl and mix well. Using a ring mold lined with the caul fat, form a patty. Brush with olive oil and grill to medium rare, approximately 3 minutes per side.

While burger is cooking, place the arugula, onion, olives, tomatoes, feta, dill, and mint in a mixing bowl. Dress with lemon juice and extra virgin olive oil. Season with salt and pepper. Place burger on bun, garnish with salad and serve.

CHEF / OWNER

Michael Psilakis

torta de carnitas

YIELDS 4 TORTAS

INGREDIENTS

4 deli sandwich rolls

Mayonnaise, as needed, to taste

1 red onion, thinly sliced

1 large ripe tomato, sliced

¼ lb. tropical queso (cheese), sliced ¼ inch thick

1 avocado, cut into slices, just before serving

4 pickled jalapeños (recipe follows)

1 lb. pork carnitas, (recipe follows)

4 oz. iceberg, romaine or mesclun mix

PORK CARNITAS

6 lbs. pork shoulder, cut into 1½-inch dice

3 Tbsp. crushed red pepper flakes

4½ tsp. Kosher salt

1 cup minced red onion

6 whole cloves

1 Tbsp. anise seeds

2 Tbsp. cumin seeds

3 cinnamon sticks

METHOD

Combine the ingredients and cook in 1 gallon of water over low-medium flame until the meat falls apart. Remove the pork from the liquid and allow to cool.

PICKLED JALAPEÑO

2 cups apple cider vinegar

¼ onion, sliced

½ carrot, peeled, rough chop

1 clove

½ cup water

1 bay leaf

2 cloves garlic

½ tsp. dried oregano

¼ lb. jalapeños

METHOD

Bring everything but the jalapeños to a boil. Lower the heat and add the jalapeños. Simmer until the color of the jalapeno turns pale green. Remove from the heat and cool.

ASSEMBLY

Make the tortas (sandwiches) just before serving. Split the roll and spread mayonnaise on the top half, followed by red onion, tomato and queso. Place 4 slices of avocado on the bottom half of roll. Slice 1 pickled jalapeno and spread out over the avocado. Place about 4 oz. of hot pork on top of avocado. Top the pork with the lettuce. Put the two halves of roll together. Slice down the center.

CHEF / OWNER
SUEÑOS AND LOS DADOS
Sue Torres

open-faced swordfish, portobello & smoked bacon club

PORTER HOUSE
NEW YORK

EXECUTIVE CHEF
Michael Lomonaco

YIELDS 4 SANDWICHES

INGREDIENTS

1 lb. swordfish, cut into four ½-inch
    thick steak cuts

4 large portobello mushroom caps,
    stems removed, halved horizontally

Olive oil, as needed

Fine sea salt and freshly ground
    black pepper, to taste

2 Tbsp. lemon zest

3 Tbsp. thyme leaves

½ cup mayonnaise

2 Tbsp. freshly squeezed lemon juice

¼ lb. thinly sliced smoked bacon

4 large leaves iceberg lettuce

4 slices country bread, ¾-inch thick

2 avocados, halved, pitted, peeled,
    and thinly sliced

1 beefsteak tomato, seeded and
    thinly sliced

METHOD

Brush the swordfish steaks and mushroom caps lightly with oil and season with salt and pepper. Put the lemon zest and half the thyme leaves in a small bowl and stir them together. Sprinkle the mixture over the mushrooms. Put the mayonnaise in a bowl. Add the remaining thyme leaves and the lemon juice and gently stir together. Set aside.

Preheat a sauté pan over medium high heat. Add the bacon and cook until crisp, approximately 5 minutes. Use tongs to set aside on a paper-towel lined plate.

Heat an outdoor grill or grill pan. Toast or grill the bread slices until golden. Put 1 slice on each of 4 dinner plates and set aside. Put the mushroom caps on grill. Grill until they begin to brown, approximately 2 minutes, turn over and cook on the other side for 2 minutes. Transfer to a plate and set aside. Grill the swordfish until cooked on the outside, but still medium-rare inside, 3 to 4 minutes per side. Remove the steaks from the grill.

ASSEMBLY

Place a lettuce leaf on each piece of bread and top with sliced avocado, tomato, swordfish, and bacon. Drizzle lemon-thyme mayonnaise over the top and serve.

Tarsus

RIBERA DEL DUERO
DENOMINACIÓN DE ORIGEN CALIFICADA
RESERVA

Bodegas Tarsus

black truffles & foie gras

on country bread

SERVES 4

INGREDIENTS

4 slices of French country bread,
  cut ½ inch thick

¼ lb. foie gras terrine, not too cold

4 black truffles

Freshly ground black pepper, to taste

Maldon sea salt, to taste

2 tsp. extra virgin olive oil

METHOD

Toast the country bread slices until they are golden brown in color. Cut the foie gras terrine into 4 thick slices. Put one slice on each piece of toast and carefully spread the foie gras, being sure to cover the toast entirely. Slice the black truffles 1/8 inch thick. Cover the foie gras on each piece of toast with a layer of sliced truffle. Grind black pepper over the truffles and season with Maldon sea salt. Drizzle a small amount of extra virgin olive oil over the truffles.

SANDWICHES of the WORLD

Le Bernardin

EXECUTIVE CHEF
Eric Ripert

porchetta arrosta

INGREDIENTS

1 10-lb. pork shoulder, deboned

Salt and freshly ground black pepper,
    to taste

½ cup plus 1 oz. acacia honey

½ cup rosemary, finely chopped

¼ cup garlic, finely chopped

1½ onions, julienned

2 cups white wine

2 cups brown veal stock

½ cup cider vinegar

ROSEMARY MAYONNAISE

1 cup mayonnaise

1 Tbsp. chopped rosemary

½ small red onion, minced

A splash of vinegar

Sugar, to taste

Salt, to taste

METHOD

Preheat oven to 375°. Open pork shoulder on a cutting board. Season inside with salt and pepper. Mix 1/2 cup honey, rosemary, and garlic in a bowl. Spread mixture evenly over meat. Tie the roast and season outside with salt and pepper. Place julienned onions in a roasting pan and add wine and stock. Place roast in pan, cover with aluminum foil and roast in oven for two hours. Remove foil and roast an additional 40-60 minutes or until the roast is nicely brown (Note: Add water to pan if juices dry out). Remove from oven to a platter. Cover with foil and set aside. Strain sauce through china cap, pushing the juice out of the solids. Add one ounce of honey and cider vinegar to the sauce. Reduce sauce to about 2.5-3 cups liquid. Season with salt and pepper.

METHOD

Thoroughly combine the mayonnaise ingredients.

EXECUTIVE CHEF
Vinny Scotto

truffled meatloaf

SANDWICHES of the WORLD

YIELDS 2 LOAVES

INGREDIENTS

1 medium-sized black truffle

1 cup white onion, minced

¼ cup extra virgin olive oil

4 Tbsp. kosher salt, divided

¼ Tbsp. aleppo chili flakes

¼ tsp. cayenne pepper

¾ Tbsp. ground fennel seeds

¾ Tbsp. paprika

1 cup whole milk

4 eggs

3 cups soda water

¾ Tbsp. fresh rosemary, chopped

¾ cup fresh parsley, chopped

¾ Tbsp. dried oregano

5 lbs. ground beef

1 cup grated Parmesan cheese

¾ Tbsp. ground black pepper

1 qt. panko bread crumbs

¾ cup garlic confit, puréed

METHOD

Preheat oven to 350°. Finely chop half of the black truffle and set aside. Sweat onions in extra virgin olive oil and 1 Tbsp. of salt until soft and translucent. Add the aleppo, cayenne, fennel seed, and paprika. Deglaze pan with milk and set aside to cool. Whisk in eggs. Add soda water, rosemary, parsley and oregano. Combine meat with wet ingredients, working it well with your hands to be sure there are no undressed clumps of meat. Fold in chopped black truffle, cheese, remaining salt, pepper, bread crumbs, and puréed garlic confit, a half a quart at a time until appropriate consistency is reached. Bake for 45 minutes. Cut into slices. Shave remaining half of truffle over the top and serve.

GRAMERCY TAVERN

EXECUTIVE CHEF
Michael Anthony

aleutian grilled cheese

146

YIELDS 1 SANDWICH

INGREDIENTS

3 oz. fresh Alaskan king crab meat, sliced thin

Truffle mayonnaise, to taste (recipe follows)

½ bunch sliced chives

Salt and pepper, to taste

1 oz. truffle cheese

2 slices brioche bread

1 piece crab bacon (recipe follows)

METHOD

Combine crab meat with mayonnaise to taste, chives, salt and pepper. Shred truffle cheese onto bread slices. Build the sandwich with mixed crab meat and crab bacon. In a non-stick skillet add butter and place the sandwich in the pan and sauté until golden brown on both sides.

CRAB BACON

1 cup shallots

½ cup garlic

1 bunch dill

2 qts. hot water

1 qt. white wine

38 oz. white wine vinegar

6 lemons

2 qts. sugar

1 qt. salt

1 piece king crab tail

3 Tbsp. cracked black pepper

METHOD

Combine all of the above ingredients. Marinate king crab tail in brine for 1 hour. Smoke the tail over hickory wood and then char on grill until caramelized.

TRUFFLE MAYONNAISE

4 egg yolks

1 Tbsp. chopped black truffle

Salt and pepper, to taste

2 oz. black truffle oil

3 cups canola oil

1 Tbsp. fresh lemon juice

METHOD

Combine egg yolks, chopped black truffles, salt and pepper in a mixing bowl. Slowly emulsify the oils by whisking them in at a rapid pace. Finish with lemon juice, salt and pepper.

EXECUTIVE CHEF
Derrick Styczek

tea sandwich sampler

LOBSTER SALAD

1 2-lb. Maine lobster

1 cup chopped lovage

1 mutsu apple, diced small

1 small black truffle, shaved

1 cup fresh aioli

1 small fresh pita round, baked and cooled

1 cup fresh arugula flowers

1 cup pickled shallots

1 Tbsp. chopped mint

METHOD

Separate lobster tail and claw. Poach tails for 2 minutes and claws for 6 minutes. Cool in ice water and remove from shells. Dice the tail meat and reserve claws and knuckles whole. Fold lobster meat with the lovage, apple, truffle, and the aioli. Fill the pita with the lobster salad. Garnish with arugula flowers, pickled shallot, and mint.

CRISPY SOFT SHELL

2 spears white asparagus, trimmed

2 oz. pea tendrils

Lemon juice, to taste

Extra virgin olive oil, as needed

Salt and pepper, to taste

½ cup sheep milk yogurt

2 Tbsp. white wine vinegar

1 cup farina

½ cup water chestnut starch

1 soft shell crab

Olive oil, as needed for frying

2 slices brioche

METHOD

Shave the asparagus on a mandolin and reserve. Pick through the pea tendrils and reserve. Combine the pea tendrils and asparagus and dress with lemon juice, olive oil, salt, and pepper. Combine yogurt, vinegar, salt, and pepper and reserve. Sift farina with water chestnut starch, dredge the crab, and fry in olive oil until crispy. Assemble sandwich on grilled brioche.

BOTAN EBI PRAWNS

6 pieces raw Botan Ebi

1 sea urchin

Olive oil, as needed

2 ripe tomatoes

1 sheet fresh filo dough

¼ cup of feta

Fresh chive blossom

Fresh greek oregano

1 head of green spring garlic, julienned

Orange zest, to taste

Salt and pepper, to taste

1 oz. trout roe

METHOD

Peel and clean the prawns and sea urchin and hold in olive oil. Peel and seed the tomatoes and dry in low oven over night. Roll filo around metal cylinder and fry in olive oil until crispy. Let cool completely and remove. Toss raw prawns and sea urchin with feta, herbs, garlic, and orange zest. Let sit for 15 minutes. Add tomatos. Season with salt and pepper. Gently fill the crispy filo round and garnish with trout roe.

anthos

EXECUTIVE CHEF
Michael Psilakis

CHEF DE CUISINE
Jason Hall

CHAMPAGNE
BRUT
PERRIER JOUËT
FLEUR DE CHAMPAGNE
1998
à Epernay-France

smoked trout blt

requires advanced preperation

YIELDS 1 APPETIZER

SANDWICHES of the WORLD

INGREDIENTS

4 oz. alderwood-smoked rainbow trout

1 Tbsp. warm bacon fat

1 Tbsp. soft-cooked bacon lardons

¼ oz. baby arugula

3 quarters of roasted tomato
   (recipe follows)

3 triangles of thin brioche toast

1 Tbsp. aioli (recipe follows)

AIÒLI (GARLIC MAYONNAISE)

3 egg yolks

1 tsp. sea salt

1 Tbsp. champagne vinegar

1 Tbsp. garlic confit

2 cloves fresh garlic, minced

1 cup peanut oil

2 cups extra virgin olive oil

2 Tbsp. heavy cream

ROAST TOMATO

6 ripe plum tomatoes, cut lengthwise into quarters

Sea salt and black pepper, to taste

¼ cup garlic confit (whole garlic cloves cooked
   until soft in olive oil)

¼ cup thyme leaves, picked, cleaned and crushed

METHOD

Place the first 5 ingredients in a food processor. While the blade is spinning, pour the oils in very slowly in a small steady stream. Add the cream and taste to correct the seasoning. Let the mayonnaise sit in a refrigerator overnight to allow the flavors to blend and mellow. Makes 3 cups aiòli.

METHOD

Preheat oven to 500°. Season the tomatoes with salt and pepper. Mix the garlic and thyme and smear each cut side of tomato. Shut the oven off. Place the prepared tomato wedges on a baking sheet pan and roast for 8 hours in the pre-heated oven. Remove and refrigerate to store. Makes 24 pieces of roast tomato.

METHOD

Hot-smoke trout filets for 5 minutes over burning alderwood chips in a metal box smoker. Remove and skin filets, being careful to remove all bones. Arrange the trout pieces on a plate. Spoon bacon fat and lardons over the fish. Arrange the remaining ingredients around the fish on the plate.

WAYNE NISH

Capuchino
Very Rare Palo Cortado
Type Dated Sherry of more than
30 years V.O.R.S.
Sherry
750 ml   PRODUCED AND BOTTLED BY PEDRO DOMECQ, JEREZ DE LA FRONTERA, SPAIN   20 % alc/vol

pork belly and green apple sandwich

SERVES 2

PORK BELLY

4 oz. pork belly

1 sprig rosemary, chopped

2 lemons, zested

Salt, to taste

POTATO CRISPS

1 large russet potato

Clarified butter, as needed

Salt, and pepper to taste

APPLE

1 green apple

1 lemon, juiced

1 Tbsp. olive oil

2 Tbsp. micro chives

Salt, and pepper to taste

Green apple mustard, as needed

METHOD

Marinate the pork belly with chopped rosemary and lemon zest. Season with salt. Rest in the refrigerator for 12 hours. Seal the pork in a vacuum pack. In a large pot, heat water to 133°; add pork; cook for 48 hours, keeping temperature constant and replenishing water as needed; remove; reserve warm. Slice the pork into 1/2 inch slices, 2 inches long.

Using a Japanese Sheeter, cut the potato into a long sheet. Cut the potato into 4 inch squares. Brush the potato with clarified butter, and season with salt and pepper. Lay the potato between 2 silpats and bake at 425° until golden brown, about 8 minutes.

Using a vegetable spinner, cut the apple into long julienne pieces. In a small bowl combine all the ingredients and season with salt and pepper.

Lay out 3 pieces of potato on a cutting board. Top with the julienned apple. Lay the warm pieces of pork belly on top. Place a dollop of green apple mustard. Finish by placing a potato crisp on top, forming a sandwich. Serve with additional green apple mustard on the side.

DANTE

EXECUTIVE CHEF
Dante Boccuzzi

bocadillo de jamón y queso con tortilla

ham and cheese sandwich with potato and egg omelette

YIELDS 6 SANDWICHES

PAN CON TOMATE

6 pieces of bagette, cut in half
    lengthwise and toasted

1 garlic clove

6 very ripe tomatoes, halved

Arbequina extra virgin olive oil, as needed

Maldon salt, to taste

METHOD

Rub the toast with a garlic clove.
Rub the flesh and seeds of the
tomatoes into the toast, discarding
the skin. Drizzle with the olive oil
and sprinkle with salt.

TORTILLA CATALANA

1 medium onion, finely chopped

Olive oil, as needed

6 medium baking potatoes, peeled
    and cut into ⅛ inch slices

Salt and pepper, to taste

12 large eggs

2 cloves garlic

2 Tbsp. chopped parsley

METHOD

Slowly sweat the onion in oil. Once translucent, remove and
cool. Place slices of potato in olive oil and simmer. Add salt and
pepper. Cook until tender but do not brown. Remove and cool.
Beat the eggs and add salt and pepper. Combine eggs, onion,
potatoes, garlic and parsley. Mix well.

Off the stove, fill a well oiled non-stick skillet with the potato
and egg mixture. Place the pan on low heat, cooking slowly.
With a rubber spatula, free the tortilla around the edges. After
20 minutes, when the eggs are cooked, flip and cook the other
side for 10 minutes. Flip and cook again for another 5 minutes.

SALSA ROMESCO

½ cup toasted almonds

12 piquillo peppers

1 small jalapeño pepper, minced

½ cup extra virgin olive oil

10 cloves garlic, minced

2 sprigs parsley, minced

½ cup toasted breadcrumbs

2 Tbsp. red wine vinegar

Salt, to taste

1 lb. thinly sliced Serrano ham

1 lb. 12 month old Manchego
    cheese, sliced

Blend almonds in a blender or food processor. Remove and
then blend piquillo peppers separately. Combine all of the
ingredients in a bowl, mixing thoroughly.

To assemble, slice the tortilla into wedges and place on the
bottom half of the pan con tomate. Cover tortilla with salsa
romesco. Add sliced ham and sliced manchego. Finish with
the top half of the pan con tomate and press. Slice on an
extreme diagonal.

BAR *jamón*

EXECUTIVE CHEF
Andy Nusser

truffle grilled cheese
with pomme soufflé and bacon foam

INGREDIENTS

3 slices aged cheddar

2 slices Swiss cheese

2 slices white bread

1 tsp. butter

Sliced truffles, as needed

METHOD

Place all the cheese between the white bread. In a sauté pan melt the butter and cook the bread on both sides till golden brown. Cut into perfect squares and garnish the grilled cheese with thin slices of truffles.

POMME SOUFFLÉ

1 Idaho potato

3 cups oil

Salt, to taste

METHOD

Peel the potato and cut the outside into the desired shape. Slice the potato into 1/8 inch slices and soak in cold water. Let the potato dry on a towel them and fry for 2 minutes in 300° oil, shaking the pan often. Remove the potato and fry in 375° oil for 2 more minutes until the potato puffs up. Remove from oil and season with salt immediately.

BACON FOAM

½ lb. bacon, diced

1 cup heavy cream

Salt, as needed

Chervil, to taste

METHOD

Render the fat out of the bacon and set the crisps aside. Add the cream to the bacon and season with salt. Place the cream mix into a foam canister and add CO_2 cartridges. Foam the bacon cream into a small bowl. Take the bacon crisps and dry them out in a 200° oven for 2 hours. Blend the bacon pieces until small. Use as a garnish with some pieces of chervil.

Pantry Raid Style

CHEF

Michael Schulson

applewood smoked bacon-glazed scallops
with butternut squash risotto pancake

GLAZE FOR SCALLOP

1 12-oz. bottle maple vinegar

2 cloves garlic

1 one-inch piece of ginger, peeled

1 cinnamon stick

2 shallots, sliced

½ a nutmeg

3 cloves

1 star anise

4 oz. maple butter

METHOD

Combine and cook all of the above ingredients except the butter until reduced to a half cup. Strain, and then add 4 oz. maple butter.

PRINCE ST. CAFE

EXECUTIVE CHEF
Gary Volkov

BACON

¼ lb. Applewood smoked bacon, diced into ½ inch pieces

½ lb. soft butter

BUTTERNUT SQUASH RISOTTO

1 shallot, small dice

2 garlic cloves, small dice

2 Tbsp. olive oil

1 cup Arborio rice

¼ cup dry white wine

4 cups juice from 5 lbs. butternut squash

Salt and pepper, to taste

Grated nutmeg, to taste

PANCAKE

1 cup flour

2 Tbsp. baking powder

Salt and pepper, to taste

2 eggs

¾ cup milk

2 Tbsp. melted butter

SCALLOPS

8 jumbo scallops

Vegetable oil, as needed

Trumpet mushrooms, sautéed, for garnish

METHOD

Sauté bacon until brown. Put into food processor with 1/2 lb. soft butter until smooth. Whisk with glaze reduction. Strain.

METHOD

Sauté shallot and garlic in olive oil 2-3 minutes. On low to medium heat, add rice and coat in oil. Add wine and cook until wine reduces. Add juice from butternut squash 1 cup at a time, frequently stirring until each batch of the juice has been completely incorporated. Add salt, pepper and nutmeg. Set aside to cool.

METHOD

Sift together the dry ingredients. In another bowl combine the wet ingredients. Mix the wet and the dry ingredients. Fold into the risotto. Mold pancakes into desired shape.

METHOD

Sear scallops on both sides in very hot oil. Remove from heat, plate, and spoon glaze over them. Add one pancake. Garnish with sautéed trumpet mushrooms and salad of your choice.

chicken katsu sando
chicken cutlet sandwich

SANDWICHES of the WORLD

SERVES 2

INGREDIENTS

2 pieces chicken leg or breast
   (or preferred meat)

¼ tsp. salt

⅛ tsp. pepper

⅛ cup flour

1 egg, beaten

½ cup panko bread crumbs

Vegetable oil, for frying

4 oz. cabbage

Shichimi togarashi, as needed*
   (seven spice chili mix)

Tonkatsu sauce, as needed*

Butter, as needed

4 slices white bread
   (or preferred bread)

Can be bought at any Asian grocery

METHOD

If using chicken legs take bones out, otherwise take the skin off the chicken. Slice open chicken if necessary so the piece fits your bread type. Salt and pepper both sides of the chicken and lightly flour it. Dip the floured chicken in the beaten egg and then the panko. Pat well. Fry the chicken in 310-320° oil for a few minutes, turning a few times, until it turns golden brown on both sides, (usually when it returns to the oil surface). Remove to paper towels. Thinly slice the cabbage and put it in water for a few minutes, then drain (this is so the cabbage gets a crunchy texture). Mix shichimi with tonkatsu sauces and spread on both sides of the chicken. Put some cabbage on one piece of buttered bread, then the chicken, then more cabbage, and close with another piece of buttered bread. Put a plate on top of the sandwich to weigh it down for 20-30 minutes so the flavors blend. Wrap the sandwich tightly in plastic wrap and then slice it into four strips, like fingers. Wrap it in aluminum foil and place in fridge overnight.

NOTE FROM CHEF

Pork cutlet is a very popular dish in Japan, usually served with sliced cabbage and tonkatsu sauce. This is the sandwich version in chicken, since I prefer chicken, but it can be made with any meat, even fish.

NEW YORK CITY

EXECUTIVE CHEF
Nobu Matsuhisa

hoison bbq pork sandwich

requires advanced preperation

SERVES 1

INGREDIENTS

1 (5-7 lb.) Boston pork butt, bone in

METHOD

Mix all dry rub ingredients, and rub pork butt. Cover and refrigerate over night.

DRY RUB

3 Tbsp. paprika

1 Tbsp. garlic powder

1 Tbsp. brown sugar

1 Tbsp. dry mustard

3 Tbsp. kosher salt

2 Tbsp. Chinese 5 spice powder

METHOD

Preheat oven to 225°.

Score fat cap of the butt, cutting through the fat only and not into the meat.

Cook the meat 8-10 hours or until the internal temperature is 175°. Use a fork to shred the meat apart.

HOISIN BARBEQUE

3 Tbsp. Hoisin sauce

1 Tbsp. soy sauce

2 Tbsp. dry sherry

1 Tbsp. sugar

Onions, diced, as needed

Tomatoes, diced, as needed

Lettuce, shredded, as needed

METHOD

Mix all the ingredients together. Then toss in the shredded pork. Heat in a sauté pan until hot. Place on a baguette with diced onions, diced tomatoes and shredded lettuce. Serve with french fries dusted with smoked paprika.

EXECUTIVE CHEF

Joel Reiss

BRANCOTT
NEW ZEALAND

Reserve
MARLBOROUGH
SAUVIGNON BLANC

vegetarian cubano
with smoked mozzarella, dandelion, crushed beans and roasted onion

164

INGREDIENTS

1 medium red onion, cut into 5 slices

4 Tbsp. extra virgin olive oil,
　　plus extra as needed

1 bunch dandelion

Salt, to taste

1 cup cooked mixed shell beans

4 five-inch pieces of focaccia

1 dill pickle, sliced into 8 thin bias cuts

1 jalapeño, sliced thin

8 oz. smoked mozzarella

2 cloves garlic, sliced thin

METHOD

Pre-heat oven to 400°.

Sauté the onion in 1 Tbsp. of the olive oil over high heat until it starts to sizzle. Remove from heat, cover with foil and place in oven until onions are tender, about 20 minutes. Remove from oven and let sit covered until they are cool to the touch.

While the onions are cooking, rough cut the dandelion greens and place them in a bowl with cold water. Swish around to clean and let rest in the bowl until ready to cook. Heat 2 Tbsp. of oil in a large pot and add garlic. Cook garlic until lightly browned. Take pot off flame, remove dandelion from water and add to pot. Cover and return to flame, cook 1 minute, season with salt, cover and continue to cook until tender, about 4 minutes. Place onto a plate and reserve. Place beans and 1 Tbsp. of oil in a bowl, coarsely crush with a fork, season with salt and reserve.

On a heated grill or panini machine, brush focaccia with oil on both sides and toast till golden brown. Remove and cut in half.

ASSEMBLY

Spread the bottom half of the bread with the beans, then the greens, onions, pickles, jalapeño, and finally the cheese. Place the top half on and warm up the sandwich in an oven. Cut in half and serve.

Telepan

CHEF / OWNER
Bill Telepan

reverse sandwich

YIELDS 1 SANDWICH

SANDWICH

1 portobello mushroom

Salt and pepper, to taste

Olive oil, as needed

6 oz. filet mignon, trimmed and cut into two
   half-inch patties

2 oz. butter

2 slices white bread, cut with a 4 inch diameter
   ring mold

2 oz. horseradish sauce (recipe follows)

2 slices cheddar cheese (or preferred cheese)

3 arugula leaves (or substitute Bibb or peppercress)

3 slices Roma tomato (or 1 slice of a large Heirloom
   or Jersey tomato)

2 thin slices red onion

HORSERADISH SAUCE

1 cup sour cream

¼ cup chives, chopped fine

¼ cup fresh grated horseradish

1 Tbsp. cracked black pepper

METHOD

Season the portobello with salt and pepper and grill with olive oil. Cut with 4 inch round mold.

Season the filets with salt and pepper. On a hot grill, cook the steak until medium rare (or preferred temperature); set aside to cool.

In a fry pan, melt the butter over medium heat. When butter gets foamy, add the cut bread. Toast until golden on both sides and drain on paper towels.

Gather all ingredients and assemble the sandwich. Layer with a piece of filet, bread, horseradish sauce, and season with salt and cracked black pepper. Add the cheese, portobello, arugula, tomato, onion, and then dress again with horseradish dressing. Top with bread, then filet. Cut in half with serrated knife and serve.

METHOD

Mix all together and keep chilled.

EXECUTIVE CHEF

John Greeley

tuna harissa

requires advance preparation

SANDWICH

1 to 1½ lbs. fresh tuna loin, skinned and
    deboned, cut ¾" wide and 3" long

Salt and pepper, to taste

Olive oil, as needed (for searing tuna)

Fried dough, (recipe follows)

1 hard boiled egg, sliced

CURRIED LEMON

5 large lemons, cut lengthwise from
    top to bottom (but not all the way)

17½ oz. kosher salt

17½ oz. sugar

Lemon juice from 5 lemons

Tunisian harissa to taste (recipe follows)

4 Tbsp. Moroccan curried lemon (recipe follows)

1 red onion, sliced very thin

4 Tbsp. pitted Kalamata black olives, sliced

Extra virgin olive oil, as needed (for drizzling)

2 medium Yukon Gold potatoes, (recipe follows)

METHOD

In a large pot with salted water, blanch the
lemons for one minute. Strain and dry them.
In a mixing bowl, mix the lemons with the
rest of the ingredients. Transfer to a glass
jar and refrigerate for 3 weeks.

DOUGH (FRICACCE)

35 oz. all-purpose flour

1¾ oz. dry yeast

1 oz. sugar

4 oz. oil

22 ½ oz. water

2 Tbsp. brandy

1 Tbsp. salt

Oil (for deep frying)

POTATO

2 medium Yukon potatoes

1 tsp. kosher salt

HARISSA

1 lb. of spicy dry pepper

Salt, to taste

Cumin, to taste

5 cloves of garlic

METHOD

In an electric mixer bowl, place the flour, dry yeast, sugar,
oil, water, and brandy, and whisk on slow speed for 3 minutes.
Add salt and mix another 10 minutes. Transfer the dough to
a large bowl, cover with plastic wrap and let rise for 1-1¹⁄₂
hours. Transfer the dough to an oiled working surface and
divide into 12 equals pieces. Arrange the dough in an oiled
pan and let rise again for 45 minutes (you should oil the
dough to keep moist). Heat the oil to 350° and fry the dough
(about 2-3 minutes on each side) until golden brown. Remove
from oil and place on paper towels to cool.

Put the potatoes in a small pot and cover with cold water
and 1 tsp. of kosher salt. Bring to a simmer and boil gently
for 25-30 minutes (or until soft). Drain and slice to 1/2 inch
thickness. Keep warm.

Soak the pepper in cold water for a few hours (until soft).
Strain and mix with the rest of the ingredients and grind in
a meat grinder twice.

PREPARATION

Season the tuna with salt and ground black pepper. In a hot pan with olive oil, sear the
tuna for a few seconds on each side. Transfer to cutting board and slice thin. Cut the
dough from one side to the other (make a pocket). Layer the tuna, egg, harissa, curried
lemon, onion, olives and drizzle with a few drops of olive oil. Arrange the slice of potato
on top of everything.

EXECUTIVE CHEF
Efi Naon

kobe sliders
wagyu style beef on sesame brioche

SANDWICHES of the WORLD

EXECUTIVE CHEF
Michael Cressotti

INGREDIENTS

3 ½-oz. ground Kobe beef patties

3 2½-oz. sesame brioche rolls

Olive oil, as needed

Salt and pepper, to taste

3 Tbsp. spicy mayonnaise (recipe follows)

3 Tbsp. aji panca ketchup
    (or substitute regular ketchup)

3 Tbsp. shredded lettuce

3 plum tomato slices

Shishito peppers, grilled or fried,
    as needed (for garnish)

1 cup nori fries (recipe follows)

METHOD

Press ground beef into a 2 1/2 inch ring mold to form the patties. Grill sliders to the desired doneness. Toast sesame brioche on a grill with olive oil, salt and pepper. Spread one side of each roll with spicy mayo and the other side with aji panca ketchup. Top sliders with shredded lettuce and tomato. Skewer with bamboo skewer and shishito garnish.

SPICY MAYO

4 oz. mayonnaise

1 ½ oz. Tobanjan (chili garlic paste)

¼ tsp. sesame oil

METHOD

Combine all of the ingredients.

NORI FRIES

2 Idaho potatoes

Vegetable oil, as needed (for frying)

1 tsp. shichimi togarashi

1 tsp. shredded nori

METHOD

Cut potatoes into 1/2 inch x 4 inch pieces. Rinse the fries for 10 minutes to rinse out the starch. Cook in the fryer at 350°, drain and season with shichimi and nori.

steak and foie gras

SERVES 6

INGREDIENTS

3 12-oz. skirt steaks

3 Tbsp. unsalted butter, softened

Fine sea salt and freshly ground pepper,
    to taste

12 ½-inch slices ciabatta, or other good
    quality French or Italian bread

¼ cup olive oil

½ cup mayonnaise

1½ cups baby arugula leaves

3 beefsteak or other large ripe tomatoes,
    cut into 12 slices

1 can (9 oz.) terrine of foie gras,
    cut into 6 slices

12 leaves iceberg lettuce

24 slices very thin sliced cooked bacon

METHOD

Preheat a barbecue or stovetop grill. Brush the steak with the butter and season with salt and pepper. Grill about 3 minutes on each side for rare. Remove from the heat and allow to rest.

Brush one side of each slice of bread with olive oil. Spread some of the mayonnaise on the opposite side.

Cut the steak on an angle, against the grain, in about 30 slices. On the mayonnaise coated side, layer 5 slices of steak, the arugula, 2 tomato slices, a slice of foie gras, a lettuce leaf, and bacon. Place the remaining slices, mayonnaise side down, on top.

Preheat a large grill pan or 2 large heavy skillets. Place the sandwiches on the grill or in the pan. Top with a heavy pot cover, or another weight, to press the sandwiches (you can use a panini grill if you have one). Cook until browned, about 2 minutes. Turn sandwiches, cover with the weight and grill on the other side, about 2 minutes more. Cut each sandwich in half and serve hot.

BISTRO LAURENT TOURONDEL

CHEF / OWNER
Laurent Tourondel

172

SANDWICHES of the WORLD

sandwich of confit of veal breast

VEAL BREAST

½ milk fed veal breast

Salt and pepper, to taste

2 qts. of veal stock

1 btl. of white wine

10 whole shallots, peeled

2 heads of garlic, peeled

1 spring of fresh thyme

2 bay leaves

1 tsp. black peppercorns

Olive oil, as needed,
  for browning veal cubes

METHOD

Set oven to 500°. Season the veal breast with salt and pepper. Place in a roasting pan, and roast for 20 minutes. Reduce oven heat to 300°. Add all the remaining ingredients, except the olive oil. Cover with two layers of aluminum foil and braise for 3 hours. Let it cool for 30 minutes, and then remove cartilage and bones. Fold in half between 2 sheet pans and press with heavy weights for 12 hours in refrigerator. Meanwhile, strain braising liquid and reserve. In a saucepot add the braising liquid and bring it to a simmer, skimming off any scum as it reduces in consistency.

Remove pressed breast, cut in 2 x 2 inch cubes and set aside. Place large ovenproof sauté pan on high heat and add a thin layer of olive oil. Brown the cubes on all sides, and then place the pan in a pre-heated 450° oven for about 5 minutes. Remove from the oven and immediately place them in the saucepot with the braising liquid and braise for 5 minutes.

TOMATO CONFIT

4 tomatoes

Olive oil, as needed

Salt and pepper, to taste

METHOD

Wash and peel the tomatoes. Cut in half and remove seeds. Place in a sheet pan, drizzle olive oil, salt, and pepper. Baked in oven at 325° for 15 minutes. Remove and reserve.

HORSERADISH CREAM

½ cup crème fraiche

½ cup sour cream

½ cup mix chopped chive, sage,
  parsley, tarragon and thyme

1 pinch of cayenne

¼ cup mustard

3 Tbsp. fresh horseradish

METHOD

Mix all the ingredients together until you reach a creamy consistency. and reserve in the refrigerator.

SANDWICH

1 fresh baguette,
  cut in four equal parts

Butter, as needed

1 bunch of arugula

ASSEMBLY

Sauté the baguette in a pan with brown butter. When ready, spread the horseradish cream. Top with a piece of veal breast. Place the tomato confit on top of the veal and add some salt and pepper. Cover with the arugula and close the sandwich.

Fleur de Sel

EXECUTIVE CHEF
Cyril Renaud

LINDAUER
BRUT

striped bass sandwich

INGREDIENTS

1 roasted red bell pepper, sliced

1 roasted yellow bell pepper, sliced

1 bunch arugula

Micro greens, dressed

1 to 2-lb. bass, skin cooked to crisps
    between silpat

Vinaigrette

VINAIGRETTE

Ice wine (from Canada)

2 cups Muscat vinegar

2 cups blend oil

¼ cup honey

1 cup shallots, minced

1 cup chives, chopped

2 Tbsp. lemon zest

1 lemon, juiced

Salt and pepper, to taste

METHOD

Skin bass and reserve skin. Slice bass very thin. Peel and roast peppers. Place skin on sheet pan between 2 silk pads. Bake at 350° until crispy. Place sashimi, peppers, arugula, and micro greens on one piece of crispy skin. Repeat. Top with vinaigrette and then skin.

Combine ingredients and mix well.

davidburke & **donatella**

EXECUTIVE CHEF
Eric Hara

washu strip loin
with pan-fried rice bun

BURGER

1 medium onion, chopped

3 cloves garlic, chopped

Olive oil, as needed

Salt and pepper, to taste

24 oz. ground washu strip loin

3 cups cooked Japanese rice

2 oz. matsutake mushroom

4 slices tomato

Lettuce, as needed

DAIKON SLAW

2 cups daikon, julienned

¼ cup carrots, julienned

½ cup rice wine vinegar

¼ cup sugar

Salt and pepper, to taste

Chopped chives, as needed

CONDIMENTS

Soy sauce

Grated wasabi

METHOD

Sauté the onions and garlic in olive oil until the onions are translucent. Season with salt and pepper. Transfer to a bowl and mix with ground washu. Season with salt and pepper and shape into patties. Form cooked rice into desired shape and pan fry on both sides until crisp. Grill matsutake mushrooms and slice thin. Sauté washu burger to desired doneness and arrange on rice bun with tomato, mushroom, and lettuce.

METHOD

Combine the ingredients for the daikon slaw in a non-metallic bowl and season with salt and pepper.

Serve with soy sauce and grated wasabi.

NEW YORK CITY

CHEF DE CUISINE

Ricky Estrellado

lobster club sandwich

ROASTED PEPPER MAYONNAISE

4 room-temperature egg yolks

1 Tbsp. Dijon mustard

1 Tbsp. red wine vinegar

Salt and pepper, to taste

1 cup grape seed oil

3 cups vegetable oil

2 medium red peppers, roasted,
    skins and seeds removed, chopped

1 bunch fresh tarragon, chopped

METHOD

Place the egg yolks, mustard, red wine vinegar, salt and pepper in a stainless steel bowl. With a whisk, incorporate the oils in a thin stream. Add the chopped peppers and tarragon to the mayonnaise. Check seasoning, keep aside for use.

INGREDIENTS

Salt, as needed

1 cup red wine vinegar

2 1½-lb. lobsters

Black pepper, to taste

Lemon juice, as needed

2 cups roasted pepper
    mayonnaise (recipe on left)

2 Yukon potatoes

Vegetable spray, as needed

1 head red leaf or Boston lettuce

2 ripe mangoes

6 slices cooked bacon

2 medium sized red tomatoes, sliced

1 box micro greens or 2 handfuls
    baby greens

Olive oil, as needed

METHOD

In a sauce pot, bring 4 quarts of water to a boil. Add salt and 1 cup red wine vinegar. Boil lobsters 8-10 minutes and transfer to an iced bath. When cooled, shell the lobsters and slice into 1/4 inch slices, including the claws. Season with salt, pepper, lemon juice, and 4 Tbsp. roasted pepper mayonnaise. Refrigerated.

Peel and slice the mangoes into 1/4 inch slices by placing the flat sides of the mango on a mandolin. Set aside. Peel the potatoes and cut into paper thin slices on a mandoline or a slicing machine. Do not wash them. There should be enough potato slices to make 3 crisps. Spray the bottom of a 6 inch, non-stick, oven-proof skillet egg frying pan with vegetable cooking spray and arrange the potato slices staggered until the bottom of the pan is covered. Bake at 375° for 12 to 15 minutes or until golden brown. Remove from oven and let cool. Repeat twice to make three crisps. Wash and spin the lettuce and set aside.

ASSEMBLY

Place one potato crisp on a plate and spread evenly with mayonnaise, repeat the same with other 2 potato crisps. Arrange the lobster slices over first potato crisp, then the mango slices, another potato crisp, mayonnaise side down, then the lettuce, bacon and tomato and the 3rd potato crisp. Season the micro greens with salt, pepper, lemon juice and olive oil. Toss and place atop the sandwich.

NORMA'S

EXECUTIVE CHEF

Emile Castillo

peanut butter, white chocolate on banana toast

PULLA (COFFEE BREAD)

½ package dried yeast

¾ oz. fresh yeast

⅔ cup milk

1 egg

1 tsp. salt

½ cup sugar

½ Tbsp. crushed cardamom

1 lb. all-purpose flour

3½ oz. butter

1 beaten egg, as needed (for egg wash)

METHOD

Dissolve the yeast in luke-warm milk. Beat the egg and add to the liquid. Mix in the salt, sugar, cardamom and flour and beat well. Soften the butter or margarine and add it to the other ingredients. Knead the dough until it separates from the sides of the bowl. Let the dough stand at room temperature for about half an hour. Form into small rolls or long loaves. Let rise. The bread is ready for the oven when you press the surface and the depression bounces back. Brush with beaten egg. Bake loaves at 400° for 20-25 minutes or the rolls for 5-10 minutes.

WHITE CHOCOLATE PASTRY CREAM

(Yields 2 cups)

1 cup milk

2 oz. sugar, divided

1 oz. white chocolate

3 oz. butter

¾ oz. cornstarch

1 egg

1 egg yolk

1 cup peanut butter

1 Banana

METHOD

Combine milk, 1/2 the sugar, white chocolate and butter in a sauce pan. Bring the mixture to a boil. Stir together the remaining sugar and cornstarch. Add the egg and egg yolk to the sugar-cornstarch mixture and blend well. Add a little of the boiling milk mixture to the egg mixture, constantly whisking, to temper the eggs. Slowly pour in the egg mixture, while whisking back into the boiling milk mixture. Return the pastry cream to a second boil. While the white chocolate mixture is warm, blend with peanut butter.

Slice the banana onto a cookie sheet. Sprinkle with sugar and caramelize with a torch or under a broiler.

ASSEMBLY

Toast a thick slice of pulla. Place peanut butter and white chocolate mixture in a pastry bag. Pipe onto bread. Dot with the caramelized banana slices.

Pine Hollow
Country Club

EXECUTIVE CHEF
Ari Nieminen

beijing peach

INGREDIENTS

2 oz. jasmine green tea
   infused vodka*

1 oz. white peach puree

½ oz. fresh lime juice

¾ oz. simple syrup

1 pansy

METHOD

Shake with cubed ice and strain into a cocktail glass.

* To infuse vodka, place 2 tablespoons of Jasmine Pearls into a container and muddle them to break them up. Pour one bottle of vodka over the tea and let sit for 4 hours. Strain the vodka through a fine tea strainer to remove all of the tea. With a funnel, put vodka back into its original bottle for easy use.

MIXOLIGIST
Julie Reiner

strawberry panino

continued from page 34

ITALIAN SPONGE CAKE
(GELATO DI FRAGOLE)

1 cup heavy cream

1 cup whole milk

½ cup plus 1 Tbsp. granulated sugar

Half of one vanilla bean

6 large egg yolks

½ lb. cleaned, sliced strawberries

An additional 3 Tbsp. granulat sugar

RISTORANTE
BaBBO
ENOTECA

CHEF / OWNER   PASTRY CHEF

Mario Batali   Gina DePalma

METHOD

Place the heavy cream, milk, and 1/2 cup of the sugar in a heavy-bottomed saucepan. Scrape the vanilla bean and add the seeds and bean pod to the pot, and place over medium heat. Meanwhile, whisk the egg yolks well with the remaining tablespoon of sugar in a large bowl. When the milk/cream mixture comes to a boil, remove the pan from the heat. Add a splash of the hot liquid to the bowl with yolks, and immediately begin to whisk vigorously. Slowly whisk in the remaining liquid, then return the entire mixture to the saucepan and continue to whisk for about a minute or so. Strain the gelato base through a chinois or fine-meshed sieve to remove any bits of cooked egg.

Allow the gelato base to cool completely in the refrigerator, whisking occasionally so it will cool evenly. While the gelato is cooling, place the cleaned strawberries in a blender or food processor along with the additional 3 Tbsp. of sugar. Pulse to achieve a chunky puree, but do not over process or the strawberries will liquefy. Stir the strawberry puree into the cold gelato base to thoroughly combine them. Immediately transfer the gelato to an ice cream freezer and freeze according to manufacturer's instructions.

In a heavy-bottomed sauté pan, melt the 1 Tbsp. of unsalted butter until it sizzles and add the 2 Tbsp. of olive oil. Gently place the slices of sponge cake into the pan, and sauté them until they are golden brown on the outside, turning them once to brown them evenly. Add more oil and/or butter to pan if necessary; the cake may absorb it. Drain the cake slices on paper towels and then dust them with confectioner's sugar.

Soften the strawberry gelato until it is spoonable and spreadable.

ASSEMBLY

Cut the cake slices in half, straight or on the diagonal. Place one half on two dessert plates and top each with a scoop of softened gelato, pressing the gelato to cover the surface of the cake. Toss the 1 cup of strawberries with the 2 tsp. granulated sugar. Top the gelato with about 1/4 cup of sliced strawberries, spooning over their juices. Place the second half of the cake on top, and repeat with the gelato and strawberries. Drizzle the strawberries with a few drops of the aged balsamic vinegar. Top each panino with the remaining cake half-slices, dusting with additional confectioners sugar. Garnish each panino with a few sliced strawberries and serve immediately.